G

TEN HEROES OF THE TWENTIES

It was a time of dance marathons and flagpole sitting, a time of get-rich-quick and Arctic exploits, a time of airplane triumphs and a "monkey trial" in Tennessee.

It was the roaring, riotous, frenzied decade in American history and it was filled with any number of heroes. Ten of those heroes are set down here in amusing and penetrating vignettes. Babe Ruth, the home run king, Ernest Hemingway, writer for the lost generation, Clarence Darrow, the wonderful lawyer, are three who helped to change a decade.

All offered romance, adventure and liveliness to an excitement-hungry people. All were as colorful as the decade that nurtured them. Rex Lardner brings the heroes as well as the flavor of the period into focus.

BABE RUTH, Home Run King

ERNEST HEMINGWAY, Writer

ADMIRAL RICHARD E. BYRD, Polar Explorer

CHARLES A. LINDBERGH, Aviator

J. EDGAR HOOVER, Lawman

JACK DEMPSEY, Fighter

BILLY MITCHELL, Air Force Leader

AMELIA EARHART, Queen of the Skies

CLARENCE DARROW, Lawyer

GEORGE GERSHWIN, Composer

Ten

Heroes

of the

Twenties

By Rex Lardner

G. P. Putnam's Sons   **New York**

12 up

Contents

10 HEROES OF THE TWENTIES

INTRODUCTION

They were the bustling, roaring, riotous Twenties, the ten-year span that contained more color, more excitement, more frenzied foolishness than any decade before or since.

The beginning and the end were neatly marked. In 1920, America, having emerged triumphant from a large-scale war, began to feel its muscles as an important world power. Following a brief period of strikes and a minor depression, the nation launched into an era of unparalleled prosperity — and then came the greatest stock market crash in history. The good times were suddenly over.

On the serious social level, it was a period of revolution — in dress, manners, morals, sophistication, scientific achievement, living standards; on the more frivolous level, it was get-rich-quick time, a time for frolicking and seeking thrills. It was as though the nation, suddenly gifted with a hyperthyroid vitality, had become engaged in a search for the Bluebird of Happiness and sought it in implausible ways. This was the Jazz Age, the Era of Wonderful Nonsense, the Lawless Decade and the Golden Age of Sport — all wrapped up in one glorious red-white-and-blue package.

"It was like a children's party taken over by the elders," novelist F. Scott Fitzgerald was to recall.

The party did not lack for amusement to watch or take part in: dance marathons, flagpole-sitting, rocking-chair marathons, contests to determine who could stay in a tree the longest. A young man played his harmonica continuously for three and a half hours, presumably a record. Another young man spun a yoyo (a toy imported from the Philippines) over a hundred thousand times. People ate gingko roots for their health, played mah-jongg, and at the behest of Émile Coué, repeated, "Every day in every way I am getting better and better."

They danced the fast-stepping Charleston, burning off a little of their energy. With regularity and with sly glee, they broke the Eighteenth Amendment — one of the most disastrous pieces of legislation ever passed by lawmakers. Most of them tolerated, and a few admired, the gangsters who reaped huge profits from the people's desire for something forbidden. The language profited by incorporating such words as speakeasy, rumrunner, bootlegger and typewriter — for machine gun.

Women, emancipated politically by the Nineteenth Amendment, achieved emancipation in other areas. They smoked in public, exchanged black lisle stockings for flesh-colored silk, bobbed their hair and dressed more comfortably. A symbol of the era was the flapper with her unfastened galoshes, cloche hat, low-waisted dress and pencil-slim look. Her counterpart was the sheik (so-called after a movie made by the smoldering Rudolph Valentino). The sheik wore, not a burnoose but a raccoon coat and bell-bottom trousers, and his plastered-down hair shone like a mirror.

It was a time of laissez-faire on all levels. The Federal Government left businesses alone; city officials let gangsters operate as they pleased; and the voters paid little attention to the shenanigans of the Warren G. Harding Administration, which turned out to be the most corrupt in American history. Harding's successor, Calvin Coolidge, was content to do nothing to change the status quo insofar as businessmen and investors were concerned. Since the country was producing things like autos and radios at a great rate and since persons both high and low were buying them (on the installment plan), who was to criticize him?

It was an age of thrills — to read about, marvel at, or experience: aerial circuses, dirigible flights, tours over terrible roads in Reos, Moons and Stutzes, gigantic ticker-tape parades, the glorious funeral of Chicago gangster Jim Colosimo, the tear-ridden funeral of Valentino, picking up New Zealand or South America on the mysterious radio, delighting in the social graces of gangster Al Capone. You could marvel at the wealth of the movie folk and shudder over the bad ends some of them met: director William Desmond Taylor, who was mysteriously murdered; actor Wallace Reid, who died of narcotics; and comedian Fatty Arbuckle, whose career was ruined by scandal.

There were other shudder-provoking events: the murder of young Bobby Franks by Leopold and Loeb; the St. Valentine's Day gang-slaying in Chicago; the tragic trial and execution of Sacco and Vanzetti; and the bizarre Snyder-Gray murder case. Another trial that received national prominence was that of John Scopes, who was accused of teaching students a theory contradicting statements

11

in the Bible — the "Monkey Trial" in Dayton, Tennessee.

Furnishing drama in the sports arena were the most colorful and explosive athletes of any era: Jack Dempsey, who could break a man's jaw with a single punch; Babe Ruth, who could hit a baseball harder and farther than any man alive; Bill Tilden, the amateur tennis champion, with his cannonball serve and fiery temper; Walter Hagen, who beat his golf opponents with psychology, and Bobby Jones, who beat them by applying relentless pressure; Ty Cobb, who awed pitchers with his batting skill and frightened basemen with his flying spikes; Red Grange, the Illinois halfback who could dodge his way through eleven tacklers and score touchdowns at will; plucky Gertrude Ederle, the first woman to swim the English Channel; Knute Rockne, the indomitable Notre Dame football coach; and Helen Wills, Willie Hoppe, Tommy Hitchcock, the original Boston Celtics and the great racehorses Man O' War and Exterminator.

The era was one filled with lively, romantic, adventurous individuals, and Americans had a vast choice of heroes to honor. The lives of ten of them are set down here:

The two most celebrated sports figures of the era, Babe Ruth and Jack Dempsey.

Ernest Hemingway, the foremost spokesman for the wistful, disillusioned Americans of the time.

J. Edgar Hoover, who best typifies the early efforts of the Federal Government to fight organized crime.

Clarence Darrow, the wise, stubborn, compassionate attorney who figured so dramatically in the trial of Leopold and Loeb and the Scopes trial.

George Gershwin, whose syncopated rhythms raised the jazz of the Jazz Age to classical status while entertaining millions.

INTRODUCTION

And finally, four persons concerned with aviation, certainly the most important scientific advance of the time: Charles A. Lindbergh, who dramatized the safety and practicability of the airplane by his flight across the Atlantic; Richard E. Byrd, who demonstrated the immutable link between the airplane and exploration; Amelia Earhart, the first great woman flier, who showed that courage and love of adventure were not the sole provinces of men; and Billy Mitchell, the dedicated prophet who, almost alone among his contemporaries, foresaw the effect of the airplane on widely held theories of military science and martyred himself in an effort to be heard.

In a period of frivolity and personal pleasure-seeking, they overcame odds, discouragement and despair to accomplish worthwhile ends. The country is greatly in their debt.

BABE RUTH
Home Run King

Free-spending, jolly, impulsive, sentimental Babe Ruth. He could eat a quart of ice cream for dessert. He once celebrated the signing of a contract by consuming an entire custard pie.

Ruth, the national hero, showed many weaknesses of the common man. When he had money, he lived high. While his fellow Yankees of the Twenties paid $3 a night for a hotel room, the Babe lived in a $100-a-day suite. He was surrounded by laughing, flattering friends who continually took advantage of his jovial willingness to pick up a check.

On short road trips, he often chose not to travel with the team but drove a sleek Packard roadster painted fire-engine red, and he drove like a fireman. One day in 1921, rocketing toward Philadelphia from Washington, D.C., he hit a turn too fast; the car shrieked into a long skid, with Ruth

15

fighting the wheel, then flipped over on its back. The Babe bounced out of the car as it rolled, landing unhurt on the cobblestones.

A newspaper printed a banner headline reporting that he was dead. But he was healthy enough, that afternoon, to hit one of his specialties against the Philadelphia Athletics. The car was a complete wreck, so he bought another one — same color.

Raised to play ball in an era when bean balls were thrown with great frequency, when players' shins were crisscrossed with nasty spike wounds, and when insults from the opponents' bench were aimed at causing blind rages in the listener, Ruth developed a keen-edged temper. Sometimes he took it with him off the ball field. One afternoon in Boston he stopped his car in the middle of the street and abandoned it while he clambered out and chased after a pedestrian who had called him a name he resented: "Two-head." The Babe had a large, round head, knew it, and did not like to hear references to its size.

"I admit I have rabbit ears," he confessed, alluding to the fact that the insults of fans and ballplayers bothered him. He climbed up into the seats after more than one fan — though the rules expressly prohibited it. Ruth chased one heckler clean out of the stadium before losing him in the parking lot; the man scooted off in such a hurry that he left his shoes under his seat. Another fan whisked a long, sharp knife out of his jacket as the Babe charged him. Ruth was happy to be held back by a couple of teammates. A year later, one teammate snapped at by Ruth for not hustling, and took a swing at him. Ruth fell down over some bats. Another — a rookie or "busher" — gave him a black eye in the locker room. Ruth did not win all his fights.

A newspaper reporter who had called Ruth yellow when

Ruth sat out three games of the Yankee-Giant World Series of 1921 held up his typewriter to protect himself when Ruth leaped into the press box to confront him, dark eyes ablaze. But Ruth was not going to hit him; he only showed him the ugly abscess on his arm that a doctor was treating. Playing was agony for the Babe. The reporter apologized.

In June, 1917, when Ruth was twenty-two and was considered a fine left-handed pitcher rather than a slugger, his temper got him into the record books in an odd way. He was pitching against the Washington Senators' lead-off man in the first inning. The umpire, Brick Owens, called three of Ruth's first four pitches balls. Ruth, who thought at least two of them were over the plate, began to steam. When the fifth pitch was called outside, giving the batter a walk, he rushed up to the plate and accused the umpire of not being able to see straight.

"One more word out of you," barked Owens, "and you're out of the ball game."

"Throw me out and I'll knock you flat!" bellowed the Babe.

Owens jerked his thumb in a gesture of dismissal. "Off the field!" he shouted.

Ruth swung and hit him in the jaw. Red Sox players swarmed around the pair and hustled Ruth to the clubhouse before he could do anything worse.

The pitcher who replaced Ruth, Eddie Shore, thereupon pitched a no-hit game. For his indiscretion, Ruth was fined $100 and suspended for ten days. Today, a player who hit an umpire would probably be banned from baseball for life.

Ruth was a master of off-the-field relaxation, and he had prodigious energy. Sometimes he would be out all night, look dead while in the locker room, then completely recuperate when the umpire cried, "Play ball!" Managers

17

who thought his nighttime antics would hurt his effectiveness as a ball player had him shadowed by private detectives. They hired bellhops to report the time he returned to his hotel. Once, the Red Sox manager burst into Ruth's room just after Ruth had come in — around dawn — and found Ruth awake and fully clothed under the covers. The Babe was smoking a pipe.

"What are you doing, smoking a pipe at this time of night?" demanded the outraged manager.

"I find it helps me relax," replied Ruth, puffing away.

When it was found that shadowing was ineffective, the Yankee management hired a detective to join the group of revelers. He pretended to be an ardent Yankee fan and escorted Ruth and a few other Yankees to night spots in various cities on the schedule. He paid for more than his share of the bills and was good company, so the players did not object when he said he wanted to shoot some pictures of them near a beer vat "for his den."

The pictures showed up in the office of the Yankee general manager. Ruth and four teammates were confronted with them and all were heavily fined.

Childlike in many ways, Ruth resented being forbidden to indulge in pleasure when the ball game was over. As the most admired sports figure of the Twenties and the highest-paid baseball player of his time, he felt he should be allowed to blow off steam to forget the pressures of trying to hit home runs to please his multitude of fans. He was consistent about it. Once, reporters happened to ask Ping Bodie, a taciturn teammate, whom he roomed with.

"Ruth's trunk," he replied.

On one memorable occasion, Ruth performed a stunt that expressed his resentment toward authority in an unusual way. During a trip west in the season of 1925 when the

Yankees were doing badly and players were on edge, the tiny manager, Miller Huggins, bawled out Ruth and out-fielder Bob Meusel for criticizing his strategy and failing to play ball as well as they could.

Ruth suddenly picked Huggins up as though he were a doll, marched with him through the observation car, and dangled him over the rail. Ruth later realized he had done a foolish thing and apologized to Huggins. He was always amazed that the little manager, who had the interests of the Yankees greatly at heart, forgave him. But Huggins was an extraordinary personality.

That was the year that Ruth had "the stomachache that was heard around the world." Just before the season opened, Ruth, feeling hunger pangs after an exhibition game in the South, stuffed himself with hot dogs and soda pop. Gulped down when he was tired and extremely hot, the meal was too much even for Ruth's iron constitution. He suffered cramps in his stomach and developed a high fever. Then, while on his way to a taxi, he pitched forward, unconscious. A teammate caught him and he was rushed to a New York hospital by train.

The effect of his illness was electric. Newspapers — even in England — flashed banner headlines. At some point Ruth had also picked up the flu bug. Radio announcers gloomily predicted that he would never play baseball again. Some newspapers reported that he was dying; others that he was dead. A London newspaper printed a flattering two-column obituary that made a pale and weak Babe chuckle when he read it.

Ruth was not out of baseball, but he got well only by slow degrees, and after he rejoined the team he played list-lessly. Because he continued to do what he pleased at night, in defiance of managerial orders, he was fined $5,000 by an outraged Huggins. It was the largest fine in the history of baseball and a move that caused a great deal of discussion among fans and in the papers. Ruth, well aware of his value to the Yankee box office if not to the baseball team, angrily appealed to the owner of the Yankees, Jake Ruppert. But Ruppert said the fine would stick and backed Huggins all the way.

Ruth apologized to Huggins and pleaded to be allowed to get into uniform. Huggins, his patience finally worn thin, refused to let him. For several weeks an extremely humble Ruth repeatedly phoned Huggins for permission to rejoin the team. Huggins eventually relented, and the Babe, weak as he was, hit the ball well in the last few weeks of that season. Without a healthy Ruth, though, the Yankees finished next to last in the American League — the worst they had done in a decade.

"Ruth is all washed up," was the consensus of many experts after his miserable season of 1925. But one of Ruth's main and most endearing characteristics was his ability to bounce back. That winter he carefully watched his diet and baked off most of the fat that had built up around his stomach. When the season opened, his eye was clear and his legs were springy. He hit 47 home runs, and with a .377 average, finished second for the batting championship of the league. "As Ruth goes," went the maxim, "so go the Yankees." The Yankees won the pennant. And millions of fans — young, old and middle-aged — were overjoyed to see their hero return.

In his twenty-two flamboyant years in the major leagues, Babe Ruth hit 714 home runs — plus 15 more in World Series play — and had a lifetime batting average of .342. He was so feared by pitchers (and the managers who gave them orders) that his record for free trips to first base will probably never be broken. He was given 2,056 bases on balls. For a slugger interested primarily in the long ball, he was a remarkably consistent hitter, winning the American League batting title in 1924 with an average of .378, and from 1920 to 1930, falling below .315 only once. In 1923, he batted a prodigious .393 — but lost the batting championship to Harry Heilmann of the Detroit Tigers, who batted .403.

In 1927, he made the most dramatic record of what is called the Golden Age of Sports — hitting 60 home runs. It was a record that stood for thirty-four years until Roger Maris of the Yankees, in a season that was 8 games longer, hit 61.

Ruth — Sultan of Swat, King of Clout, the Bambino — was the star member of the greatest baseball team ever to take the field. They were the 1927 Yankees which included formidable hitters like Lou Gehrig, Tony Lazzeri, Earle Combs and Bob Meusel. The team was so certain of exploding for a batch of runs at some point in the game that the members never worried if they fell behind. Their habit of collecting scores in the late innings earned them the nickname of Five-o'clock Lightning. The team's batting average was a record-breaking .307, and helped by four of the league's best pitchers — Herb Pennock, Waite Hoyt, Urban Shocker and Wilcy Moore — it won the American League pennant that year with the astonishing percentage of .714.

Then, just before the first World Series game, against the Pirates, Huggins tried some psychology. In pregame batting practice at Forbes Field in Pittsburgh, the Pirates were treated to an exhibition of Yankee power. In turn, Combs, Gehrig, Meusel, Mark Koenig and Joe Dugan plastered home-run balls into the stadium seats. Finally Ruth, spindle-legged, barrel-chested, cocky, walked mincingly to the plate. He dug his spikes into the dirt of the batter's box, waggled his bat at the batting practice pitcher, drew it back behind his ear and lashed out at the first offering.

There was a solid crack and the ball rocketed off the bat on a line, rising, rising until it soared completely out of the park. It was the longest hit any of the Pirates had ever seen. Understandably demoralized, they walked away, shaking their heads, and dropped the Series in four straight games.

Ruth was more than a hitter deadly in the clutches, able to change the entire complexion of a game with a single swing of his bat. He was an outfielder with a strong, accurate arm who never threw to the wrong base. He could bunt, and if a one-base hit was needed, he could place the ball in the opposite field. If he failed to hit safely, he could often be counted on to score a Yankee runner from third with a deep, towering fly to the outfield.

If his hitting talent had not prompted his being transferred to the outfield, he would have been one of the greatest southpaw pitchers who ever lived. While with the Boston Red Sox, he pitched 29⅔ consecutive scoreless innings in World Series play (1916 and 1918). It was a record not broken until Whitey Ford of the Yankees accomplished it in 1961. Ruth beat Walter Johnson, the great Washington Senators' fast-baller, in many low-scoring duels. (Ruth, who loved to hit fast balls, always hit well off Walter.) The Babe usually had Ty Cobb's number at a time when the fiery Detroit outfielder's presence at the plate was enough to frighten most pitchers out of their shoes. In 1916, Ruth had the best earned-run average of any pitcher in the American league — 1.75.

Colorful, hard-hitting, shrewd ballplayer that he was, Ruth's greatest feat goes far beyond making giant headlines or establishing records for other players to shoot at. In the early 1920s, this moon-faced, flat-nosed, uneducated fellow literally saved the game of baseball.

When Ruth became a professional, in 1914, the game was somewhat different from the one it later became. Runs were as precious as gold. Bunts, squeeze plays and stolen bases were offensive moves that a team relied on to score. The ball was relatively squashy, and hits longer than a double were considered fantastic feats of strength. Pitchers had many tricks. Not only was the spitball allowed — its eccentric path because of the weight of saliva on one side making it difficult to hit — but various specialists also doctored the ball by shining one side of it with wax, roughed up the cover with a ring or piece of emery, or discolored it with tobacco juice. Batters had difficulty in judging its flight, choked their bats in attempts to meet it, and many games at that time ended in 1-0 and 2-1 scores.

Because of World War I, the season was cut short in 1918, but the twenty-three-year-old lefty had time to cloak himself in a certain amount of fame. As a Red Sox pitcher, he won 13 games and lost 7, but as a batter he did even more impressively: his home-run total was an amazing eleven. It was good enough to tie for the American League championship. Tillie Walker of the Philadelphia Athletics also got 11. The National League king, the Phillies' Cliff C. Cravath, smashed a total of 8.

The following year, used less as a pitcher, Ruth batted .322 and poled, to the surprise of owners, pitchers and experts, 29 home runs. This was far more than enough to win the championship of both leagues and broke every home run record made in big-league baseball. At the time, Ruth contemptuously referred to the ball as being "soft as a squash."

Then, to the dismay of Red Sox rooters, he was sold to the New York Yankees, for years doormats in the American League. The price was $125,000 — the highest ever paid for a ballplayer up to that time. The Boston owner, in dire need of money, was also given a substantial loan as part of the deal.

Dominating the Yankees as he had the Red Sox in his first year, Ruth hit the astounding total of 54 home runs — a performance equal to a player's hitting 250 today. Second place in the derby went to George Sisler of the St. Louis Browns. He had 19.

Ruth's home-run total of 1920 was overshadowed by another event. This was the shocking report that eight members of the Chicago White Sox had conspired to throw the Series of 1919 to the Cincinnati Reds. The disclosure came to be known as the Black Sox Scandal.

Thinking back, fans recalled some odd things about the Series: the bitter dissension among White Sox players; the poor pitching and fielding of Ed Cicotte — known to dislike White Sox owner Charles Comiskey for what Cicotte considered his cheapness; the confused, almost comical play of a few White Sox players; rumors of a fix that had been circulating at the time; and the fact that the Reds, underdogs in the betting, had won the Series, five games to three. (The Series that year was played on a best-out-of-9 basis.)

Fans were shocked and felt betrayed. Owners were angry at the offending ballplayers. Most players, including Ruth, could not understand how their colleagues could accept money (or the promise of money — for little was ever paid) to throw ball games. Ruth was especially upset to learn that Shoeless Joe Jackson, the batter he most admired, was among those found guilty.

Baseball was hit with its severest crisis. Fearful that fans would ridicule the players and desert the ball parks in droves, baseball's owners took steps to rebuild public confidence. The eight players involved were banned from the game for life. Baseball's first commissioner was hired. This was the stern-looking, dignified, white-haired Judge Kenesaw Mountain Landis, who it was hoped would symbolize the new integrity of baseball.

Judge Landis was given sweeping powers to correct any irregularities he found and to punish and fine the breakers of rules. Rules were introduced to prevent players of opposing teams from chumming around together and to keep players from talking to customers in the stands. Landis was assured of the unswerving support of baseball's worried owners.

It is safe to say, however, that the stern-looking father image represented by Landis and the punishment of the wrongdoers were not what restored baseball to the public's affection. It was Ruth.

Fans, by their nature, are emotional people; one does not court them by appealing to their reason. They want drama, excitement and color. And Ruth gave them their fill of all of these.

"From 'One Old Cat' to the last 'At Bat,' " John Kiernan asked in a poem, "Was there ever a guy like Ruth?" Ruth was the subject of the most famous sentence in baseball journalism. It was written for the old New York *World* by Heywood Broun and went, "The Ruth is mighty and shall prevail." The reference was to Ruth's having hit two home runs against the New York Giants in the second game of the 1923 World Series. The Yankees won 4 to 2. A third blow would have been another home run had not Casey Stengel, in the Giant outfield, sprinted like a madman toward the bleachers and speared it with a flying leap just as it was about to drop in.

Was there ever a guy like Ruth? Walter Johnson called

him the hardest hitter baseball had ever seen, and the facts bear him out.

Against the Philadelphia Athletics, Ruth hit a pop fly so high that the ball faded in the clouds far above the stadium roof. Ruth trotted down to first, headed for second. The ball, hardly visible, began to plummet down in the area of second base. Jimmy Dykes, the Athletics' second baseman, his neck stiff from gazing at the ball, wandered around under it in dizzying circles. When it came back to earth, Dykes made a frantic grab for it, but it slipped through the fingers of his glove and plunked to the ground. Ruth had gotten two bases on an infield fly.

When the bewildered Dykes returned to the bench, Connie Mack, the manager, complimented him. "Good work, Jimmy," he said. "You didn't let it hit you on the head."

Once Ruth swung at a pitch thrown to him by Howard Ehmke, then with Detroit, and lashed it back so hard that if it had been a fraction of an inch to the right, it would have torn the pitcher's nose off. When Ehmke, white as a sheet, hoisted himself to his feet after jerking his face out of the way of the ball, he was quivering from his near escape.

In the fourth game of the World Series of 1926, against the St. Louis Cardinals, Ruth had one of his best days, lofting three home runs. He powdered one pitch high into the centerfield bleachers of Sportsman's Park, the ball climbing up the seats, hopping over the stadium wall and crashing into the side of a YMCA building across the street. It was the longest ball ever hit in St. Louis. In an exhibition game against the Giants in Tampa, Florida, Ruth hit a ball so far (there was no stadium to stop it) that sports writers were inspired to chase after it, locate it, and measure its distance from home plate. They found it had traveled 508 feet, the longest trip, up to then, that a batted baseball had ever made.

Sometimes Ruth hit a home run without meaning to. In a game against the White Sox, the Yankees needed one run to win. As the ninth inning rolled around, Ruth came up to bat with a man dancing off third. Realizing he was going to get nothing good to hit, Ruth choked his bat with the expectation of reaching out to poke a wide pitch between the infielders. He saw the pitch he wanted and took a quick chop at the ball. It sailed into the left-field seats.

Although it sounds incredible, in a game against the Cleveland Indians, Ruth found a nonbreaking fast ball to his liking and sent a screaming liner toward the mound that shot through the pitcher's legs and then rose until it soared over the center fielder's head for an inside-the-park home run.

Ruth's ability to hit home runs — and the fans' apparent delight in seeing them hit — changed the entire face of baseball. New rules prevented pitchers from doctoring the ball. Owners introduced a ball with more zing and bounce to it. Batters took to swinging from their heels instead of choking the bat and trying to poke the ball between infielders. Players were hired for their hitting rather than fielding ability. By the mid-Twenties, close-to-the-vest, low-scoring, bunt-sacrifice-steal baseball had given way to power baseball, runs in bunches and playing for the big inning.

When reporters and photographers gathered around the cause of all this just before a game, they were apt to ask the Babe to exhibit his swing. How he got all that power into a swish of the bat seemed a more vital question than solving the Al Capone problem, the merits of the highly disregarded Volstead Act or corruption in government.

When asked to perform, the Babe would say, "Sure, kid," (he met so many people he never bothered to learn names, even those of some of his teammates) and demonstrate.

He would plant himself on the first base side of the plate,

feet close together, shoulders slightly hunched, head out-thrust, the bat held high over his left shoulder and gripped at the very end. He held it so far down on the handle that the little finger of his left hand was hooked under the knob. The bat itself had a thin handle and a heavy barrel, almost all the weight being at the end, where the centrifugal force of his swing would do the most good. Sometimes Ruth, an exceedingly strong man, used a bat that weighed as much as 48 ounces. He had his favorites and they had names: Black Betsy, Beautiful Bella, Big Bertha.

As the pitcher performed his windup, Ruth would bring the bat back as far as possible on his twisted torso. Weight was on his left leg, his back was nearly broadside to the pitcher. Then the swing: Hurling his body around with fierce concentration, he would rapidly unwind to swing with every ounce of weight and power he owned, the bat meeting the ball with the power of an unleashed catapult. When he missed — as he was bound to do with some fre-quency — the force behind his swing sometimes caused him to lose his balance and fall to one knee.

"Once I started my swing," said the Babe, "there was no checking or stopping it. It was all or nothing." It was said of this magnetic, happy-go-lucky athlete of the Twenties that he could excite a crowd merely by striking out.

To the Japanese, who followed his career in the Twenties and Thirties and whom he visited in 1934, he epitomized everything that was American. Japanese troops who charged Americans in the jungles and on the beaches of Pacific islands in World War II expressed their defiance in an un-usual battle cry: "To hell with Babe Ruth!"

The Babe was not an orphan, as is sometimes reported, nor was he raised in an orphans' home. His father, George

Herman Ruth, of German descent, was a saloonkeeper in Baltimore, near the waterfront. Babe's father, sister and mother Kate (who died when he was thirteen) lived over it. The husky youngster's ears were assailed early by the tough talk of longshoremen and merchant sailors, and he came to accept raucous violence as a part of life.

His family worked so hard to make a go of the saloon that they did not have much time to supervise his activities or exercise much control over him. He has said that he was a bad kid — so bad that when he was a tobacco-chewing, petty-thieving seven-year-old his father placed him in St. Mary's Industrial School in Baltimore. This was a school where delinquents of a tender age, unwanted children and youngsters who ran away from home were placed to be educated and taught a trade.

Ruth was released two years later but was returned to spend four more years there. After his mother died, he stayed with his father for another year — then back he went to school. He learned how to cut and sew clothes and cobble shoes. But the most important thing that happened to young George Herman Ruth was meeting Brother Matthias. Brother Matthias was a member of the Xaverian Order — a Catholic order that specializes in helping underprivileged boys in this country and Europe.

Physically, Brother Matthias was formidable. He was six feet, six inches tall and weighed about 250 pounds. One of his major interests was baseball, and he could see, by the way young George snatched up grounders and winged the ball to basemen, that he had a knack for it. George's ability to hit had not demonstrated itself yet, but at the age of nine he played with the twelve-year-old team; at the age of twelve he played with the sixteen-year-olds, and when he was sixteen he starred on the school varsity. His specialty at the time was catching. Since the School did not have a left-hander's catcher's mitt, George would catch with his left hand, then quickly remove the mitt and throw with his left hand when he had to fire a ball to the bases.

Brother Matthias' ability to hit long flies to the outfield while swinging the bat with one hand filled George with popeyed awe. Capitalizing on the youngster's admiration, Brother Matthias taught George to read and write and explained to him the difference between right and wrong. Ruth was a quick learner under this man, whom he admired more than anyone in the world, but his natural flair for baseball made him impatient with the failures of his teammates.

One day he jeered at the pitcher because the balls he flung haphazardly toward the plate were being smacked for extra-base hits by opposing batters. Brother Matthias, annoyed by Ruth's chuckles, asked him what was so amusing.

"The pitcher." George chortled. "He's got nothing on the ball."

Brother Matthias stared down at him, his face a stern mask.

"All right, George," he said. "If you think it's so easy, *you* go in and pitch."

George complained that he was a catcher, not a pitcher.

"But you know so much about it," said Brother Matthias, "surely you can show everybody how it's done."

Reluctantly, George traded his catcher's mitt for a pitcher's glove and walked out to the box. Not knowing how to wind up or stand on the rubber, he nevertheless managed to throw the ball over the plate well enough to save the ball game. A few times he gathered up courage enough to try curving the ball, thrilled to see his pitches break as they approached the plate, and to see how they puzzled right-handed batters. These incidents convinced both Ruth and

Brother Matthias that he had the speed, control and guile to make a pitcher, and launched him on his major-league career.

How young Ruth was selected for the Baltimore Orioles of the International League is not exactly known, but the account that seems to stand up best is that Brother Gilbert of St. Mary's had promised his friend Jack Dunn of the Orioles a flashy player from St. Mary's. The Orioles of 1914 were in desperate need of new talent. Dunn asked Brother Gilbert for a player named Ford Meadows. Meadows wanted to go, but Brother Gilbert felt he should complete his schooling, so he asked Dunn to look at a slender left-handed pitcher, Georgie Ruth.

Dunn was impressed. (One story has it that Dunn never saw Ruth pitch, only saw him pick himself up off the ice after falling down, but knew immediately that he was a great athlete.) To George's astonishment, he called to him and asked, "Hey, kid, how'd you like to pitch for the Orioles?"

"Sure," said George, who thought it would be an adventure. He did not know that professional ballplayers were paid. When Dunn told him he would pay $600 a year, Ruth's mouth dropped in astonishment.

Because George was only nineteen at the time, Dunn had to agree to become his legal guardian. After the papers were signed, he took George to the Orioles' spring training camp in North Carolina. George was then over six feet tall but weighed only 160 pounds.

"You'll do a good job, George," Brother Matthias assured him as they shook hands in farewell.

A new world opened up for George. He had his first ride on a train; he met tough, hungry professional ballplayers; he was the butt of practical jokes — such as being told to rest his arm in the tiny hammock inside Pullman berths for wearing apparel. "It's for pitchers," confided a colleague. "Keep your arm there all night and you'll feel great in the morning." After a night of keeping it inside the hammock, Ruth thought his arm would fall off, it was so stiff.

He got his nickname with the Orioles. He looked so young and spanking-new when Dunn conducted him to the pitcher's mound one day, that a veteran hollered, "There goes Dunn and his new babe!" The cry was caught up by the others and the name stuck. Ruth's actions suited the name. He was so green that he used to get up early in the morning to hurry down to the station and watch the roaring trains go by. Awed by the fact that he did not have to pay for his meals, he was always first in line at the dining room for breakfast, lunch and supper. Silent, wary, he gorged himself with good things to eat like pancakes, muffins and boiled potatoes.

Ruth had never seen an elevator. He liked to ride up and down without getting out when the opportunity offered. Once he got courage enough to operate the elevator himself and stuck his head out of the door while it was descending. If a teammate had not hollered, "Look out! Pull your head in!" Ruth would have been decapitated by the edge of the floor, and American baseball history would have been written differently.

On the ball field he was not so naïve. He had a fine arm, poise and good control. At bat — for a pitcher and a rookie — the length of some of his hits made veterans blink. His poise as a pitcher was amazing. In an exhibition game against the World Champion Athletics, Ruth struck out Home Run Baker and Eddie Collins before he knew who they were. At this stage of his career he was not a brainy player, merely a strong, rugged kid who had confidence in his ability to throw harder and hit harder than his more experienced contemporaries.

Then, to Dunn's sorrow, his prize youngster had to be sold to the Boston Red Sox. Oriole attendance was suffering and Dunn needed the money. "Now you're in the majors, Babe," he said, seeing Ruth off on the train. "Show 'em that St. Mary's and I didn't make any mistake."

Ruth promised he would. He was still astonished that people got paid for playing baseball — a game he would have gladly played all day long for nothing.

With the Red Sox, he immediately got into trouble because he insisted on taking batting practice with the regulars. Sometimes he had to fight his way to the batter's cage — veterans were not going to let some pip-squeak kid take away their jobs — and sometimes he found that his favorite bats were sawed in two when it came time for him to use them. Characteristically, Ruth would pick up someone else's bat, with or without permission, and whale away with that. He had a reputation to uphold.

During his one-month stay with the Red Sox in 1914, Ruth won two games and lost one. He was up ten times and made two hits. Then he was sent to Providence in the International League — a Red Sox farm club — to help that team win the pennant over the weakened Orioles. With Providence, he hit his first home run in professional competition. The Providence manager, Bill Donovan, gave him a piece of advice he was to remember as a pitcher. "Forget about the strikeouts, kid. You've got eight players behind you. You'll last longer in baseball if you let them earn their salaries, too." Ruth nodded, and pitched well enough to be recalled by Boston.

Ruth had a good year in 1915. He had the best won-lost record of any pitcher in the American League — .750.

Sometimes used as a pinch hitter, he batted reasonably well and hit four home runs. Newspapermen, noting his go-for-broke swing and the distance the ball traveled when it connected, suggested (even at this early date) that he play daily instead of every fourth day, as he did as a pitcher. They thought he might blossom into a home-run leader — four home runs in a season being considered a remarkable total.

Thanks partly to Ruth, the Red Sox won the 1915 pennant over the Detroit Tigers and Ty Cobb, who was having an unusually good year. But Ruth did not get a chance to pitch against the Phillies, partly because the Red Sox were much the superior team. The Sox won the championship, four games to one.

In both 1916 and 1917, he won the gratifying total of 23 games for the Red Sox. More poised than ever, in one game against the Tigers with the bases loaded and none out, he fanned Ty Cobb, Sam Crawford and Bobby Veach in succession. He finally got his World Series chance in 1916, against the Brooklyn Dodgers. In a 14-inning game, the Red Sox won, two to one. The only run scored off the tireless Ruth came when two of his outfielders crashed into each other while chasing a long fly, allowing the batter an inside-the-park home run. The winning Red Sox run was scored on another fluke. Del Gainer romped home with a similar four-baser when his hit to the outfield could not be located in the dark by the frantic Dodger outfielders. The Babe gave Gainer a happy hug when he crossed the plate.

After failing to win the pennant in 1917, the Red Sox claimed it again in 1918. But the most important event of the baseball year was Ruth's gradual transfer from a pitcher to a full-time batter. Ruth had never protested when manager Ed Barrow pitched him every fourth day and had him play first base or the outfield on other days, to take advantage of his booming bat.

In the middle of the season, when Babe's home runs were making him the talk of the baseball world, Barrow called him into his office and asked him to choose pitching or batting as his specialty. It was clear that Ruth's career might be cut short if he concentrated on both: no one had ever taken a regular pitching turn and then been counted on for stellar performances in other positions on what should have been his days off. C634612 CO. SCHOOLS

"Well," said Ruth, after a moment's hesitation, "pitching is fun because I like breezing the ball past the batters — especially Cobb and Home Run Baker. But I like to play every day — and, boy, I sure like to hit that ball!" From then on, he pitched only occasionally, spending most of his time in the outfield, despite warnings by sympathetic experts that he might be killed by a high fly ball landing on his head. He found, however, that his youthful fly-shagging, with Brother Matthias hitting them out, stood him in good stead. He was soon one of the surest ground-coverers in the league.

Wilbert Robinson of the Brooklyn Dodgers was to say of him later, "That big guy has more baseball instinct than any player I ever saw. He does everything right. Always throws to the right base . . . never takes a ball off stride in the outfield. He's the greatest of them all." And he was one outfielder whose accurate arm no base runner dared take a chance on. Ruth loved to rifle the ball in from the outfield to any base.

After the 1918 season, in which he hit the astonishing (for the time) total of 29 home runs for the league championship, Ruth was sold to the Yankees. It was the best buy a ball club ever made.

Ruth started rewriting all kinds of records in New York — particularly attendance records — and his presence lifted the downtrodden Yankees to third place in the next two years and won them their first pennant in 1921.

Crowds poured through the gates to see Ruth take his vicious cut. Smashing out 54, 59 and 35 home runs, Ruth created a new kind of fan — one less interested in the fine points of the game than in seeing how hard and how far the Caliph of Clout could hit a baseball.

His feats inadvertently cost the Yankees their home. Up to 1922, the New York Giants, who owned the Polo Grounds, had allowed the Yankees to share the park while the Giants were on the road. But when it became clear that the Yankees were outdrawing the mighty Giants, the Giants invited them to go somewhere else. So the Yankee Stadium — "the house that Ruth built" — was proposed and planned in 1922 and completed in time for the first game of the 1923 season. At the time it was the world's largest baseball stadium, built to hold 60,000 spectators. But 74,000 crammed in on the day of its opening and Babe did not let them down. Perhaps inspired by President Harding, who shook hands with him and urged him to "go out and bust one," Babe did just that, hitting the first home run ever hit in the huge park.

It was while he was with the Yankees that the Ruthian color, the legends and prodigious feats grew to a point where he became the greatest sports figure of all time. Americans admired Dempsey and worshiped Lindbergh, but they loved Ruth. He had a knack for putting on performances on and off the ball field — dramatic, poignant, comic.

While the Yankees were still at the Polo Grounds Ruth used to amuse himself and early arriving fans by fungoing balls into the stands one-handed, the way Brother Matthias had slammed out long flies back at St. Mary's. After second baseman Tony Lazzeri joined the Yankees, he and Tony, brandishing scissors, used to nip holes in any teammate's socks they found lying about the locker room. Once Ruth and Gehrig commandeered a locomotive and, grinning and sooty, stoked the engine with coal and yanked the steam whistle. After the Yankees beat the Cardinals in the Series of 1928, Ruth led his exuberant teammates through the cars of the train, insisting that all males should take their shirts off. Most of them complied.

He was more superstitious than most players, who are noted for being superstitious. He never wore underwear, winter or summer, because he felt it was bad luck. He rejoiced when he saw a yellow butterfly, since that meant good luck. When the Yankees won a game, he made sure to reach the locker room by exactly the same doors he had come out of, to maintain the spell. Seeing an empty barrel on the way to the Stadium was assurance to him of a Yankee victory. To keep the gods of good fortune with the Yankees, he always touched second base as he came in from the outfield. Oddly enough, the superstitions worked more often than they didn't. While Ruth was with the club the Yankees won more pennants than any team in history, finishing first in 1921, 1922, 1923, 1927, 1928 and 1932, and being strong contenders in most of the other years.

Extremely energetic, Ruth had numberless diversions. He strummed the ukulele, blew the saxophone, and played a heady game of bridge. He liked to shoot bullfrogs at night. He gambled — losing over $125,000 — until he was taken in tow by his wife Clara and his business manager Christy Walsh. But even they could not save him from losing $100,000 in zany business investments.

The Babe accepted a $35,000 rubber check as part payment for making a potboiler movie he wished had never been filmed. In New Orleans, $1,000 fell through a hole in his pocket and was lost forever. He once got stung when a fan thrust a piece of blank paper at him for an autograph. After the Babe signed it, the fan transformed it into a modest IOU and collected on it. Ruth was paid the astounding sum of $40,000 for a vaudeville tour in 1926, but his expenses during that tour came to $50,000.

By teammates, he was suckered into a golf match with Yankee rookie Sammy Byrd, a better golfer than ballplayer. As champion of the Yankees (Ruth could hit a golf ball 350 yards), he felt disdain for Sammy and accepted all bets. Then he paid off in some bewilderment after Byrd, who later became a golf professional, swept him off the course.

In an era of crazy stunts — flagpole sitting, walkathons, dance marathons, faith healing, parties as exotic as those of the ancient Romans — some of Ruth's capers matched the wildest. He stood on top of Lookout Mountain near Chattanooga, Tennessee, and fungoed a ball half a mile away. To raise money for widows and orphans of New York policemen killed in line of duty, he caught a ball thrown from the top of the George M. Cohan Theatre on Broadway. To aid another charitable cause, he caught a ball thrown from an airplane 300 feet off the ground. He refereed a prize fight. He collected speeding tickets as though they were oil paintings. One time, thrust into jail for committing a traffic violation, the Babe enlisted the city's help, and before the game he was scheduled to play in was over, arrived at the park accompanied by a motorcycle escort whose whining sirens, along with Ruth's dramatic entrance, stopped play for fifteen minutes.

The Babe mingled — as did Dempsey, Red Grange, Bobby Jones, Bill Tilden, Gertrude Ederle, Helen Wills and other sports heroes of the time — with the most important political and social figures in the world. But the Babe was more casual about these meetings than most.

During a civic ceremony in 1921 he was introduced to the much-decorated, still-spry Marshal Ferdinand Foch, Allied Commander-in-Chief during World War I. Ruth felt he had to make a stab at conversation. "How you feeling, General?" he asked. "Were you in the war?"

He once had a date with Queen Marie of Rumania, perhaps the most glamorous of visitors to the United States in the Twenties — and stood her up.

On another occasion, Herb Pennock, the great Yankee pitcher, asked Ruth if he wanted to go out to a party.

"I can't," said Ruth. "I'm meeting a couple of people from the movies."

"Who are they?" Pennock asked, quite interested.

Ruth scratched his head. "Darned if I can remember," he said. They were Douglas Fairbanks and Mary Pickford. But Ruth skipped that date and went out with Pennock.

He still had time to do favors for everyone who asked. He hit a home run for little Johnny Sylvester, then an invalid, and did more to cure him than the doctors had been able to do. He autographed bats and baseballs for charity until his fingers cramped. He went on a country-wide tour with the St. Mary's band to raise money for new buildings. He gave Brother Matthias two automobiles.

In 1923, his kindly instincts almost got him killed. He consented to play in an exhibition game in Scranton, Pennsylvania, to raise money for orphans, and was wildly cheered when he first came to bat. He hit a home run, which threw his young fans into ecstasy. The second time up, he hit another home run, and that was all the kids could stand; they rushed onto the field — hundreds of them — and swarmed over him, knocking him down. He would have smothered to death if a cordon of police had not cut through the howling youngsters and rescued him from their grasp.

If the Babe was a national hero in 1926 he became a demigod in 1927. This was the year that pitchers had to think twice about walking Ruth because they would then face stocky Lou Gehrig, just beginning to reach his peak as a long-ball hitter. The Yankees were beating all opposition so easily (they walloped the Senators in a July 4th doubleheader 12–1 and 21–1) that fans shifted their interest to the tense race between Ruth and Gehrig for the home-run championship.

The day-by-day records were compared and speculated on. On the day Lindbergh started for Paris, May 19th, Ruth hit Number 9. When Lindbergh, wildly cheered, made an appearance at the Stadium, Ruth commemorated the event by hitting Number 22. On July 26th, both players had 31 home runs. Then Ruth surged ahead. On September 30th, he drove 70,000 fans wild by hitting 2 home runs — Numbers 58 and 59 — tying his record of 1921. Number 59 was hit with the bases loaded off the great Athletics pitcher, Lefty Grove.

In the next to last game of the season, in the eighth inning with Mark Koenig on third and one out, left-hander Tom Zachary of the Senators fed a screwball to Ruth. The ball broke in to Ruth and he swung at it, pivoting from his dainty ankles to his giant head. The ball went on a line past first base and buried itself in the screaming mob in the right-field stands. It was fair by no more than six inches. The Babe had Number 60, and Yankee Stadium exploded with hysterical noise. After the Babe jogged around the bases and crossed the plate, he paused to doff his cap with one hand and wave a salute to the fans with the other. He seemed to say, "How about *that*, folks?"

The next year, 1928, saw him have a fair season — 54 home runs, a sliding batting average of .323 — but his Series' hitting against the St. Louis Cardinals was the most astonishing ever seen. Upset by everyone's opinion that the Cardinals would have an easy time with the injury-ridden Yankees, Ruth undertook to win the Series all by himself.

Despite a bad leg and an injured shoulder, Ruth hit 3 home runs, scored nine runs and wound up with a batting average of .625. He broke or tied 19 World Series records during this splurge of hitting, and injured as he was, won one game for the Yankees by bowling over the Cardinal catcher and making him drop the ball as he tried to tag the charging Ruth. The Yankees took 4 straight games from the Cardinals in what was to be the Babe's next to last World Series.

Signs were increasing in 1929, though, that the Babe was slowing up: it took longer for him to round into shape in spring, and his legs gave him trouble; he lost several inside-the-park home runs because he did not have the wind to go past third. It was time for him to think about a less active role in the game to which he had given so much.

More mature, less headstrong in the Thirties, Ruth honestly felt that he would make a good major-league manager. He also felt, and rightly, that the Yankees owed him a great deal. More than anyone else, he had made the team the biggest attraction in baseball, as well as the richest and most successful club.

When Miller Huggins passed away in 1929, Art Fletcher, a Yankee coach, automatically stepped into the beloved Huggins' shoes, but then he turned down the job — to everyone's surprise — for the season of 1930. Ruth had an inspiration: Why not me? he asked himself. He knew pitching, batting and roaming the outfield, which made up 90 percent of baseball. Stars like Cobb, Speaker, Collins and Hornsby had graduated to managerships in their waning days; it seemed to Ruth that he was thoroughly qualified.

But Colonel Ruppert had a different point of view. He felt that Ruth's excesses in bygone years showed he was not serious enough about the game to manage others. To Ruth's great disappointment, former pitcher Bob Shawkey was appointed manager.

Ruth's salary of $80,000 was partial compensation for his being turned down for the job he wanted more than anything in the world. Shawkey did not do well enough to please Ruppert — the team finishing third — and was released.

Once again Ruth made his pitch. This time Ruppert was ready with pages of reports. He confronted Ruth with a long list of the Babe's transgressions over the years.

"Look at this, Babe," he said, showing Ruth the papers. "How can I turn my team over to you?"

Crestfallen, Ruth was unable to convince Ruppert that he had more sense now — that his experiences as a baseball playboy might enable him to understand the problems of other high-living stars. Ruth once again became a combination player and national idol, this time under Joe McCarthy, who had been let go by the Chicago Cubs after a bad season. The Babe toiled as a player for four seasons, during which the Yankees won one pennant — in 1932 — and one Series, against McCarthy's old team.

In 1933 and 1934, the end was in sight. More and more, runners were sent in for Ruth when he got on base, and in the late innings young players were substituted for him in the outfield. Partly because of the depression, his salary was sharply reduced. His last big chance came in 1934 — after his home run total sank to 22. The Tigers considered him for manager, but once again Ruth was disappointed. Mickey Cochrane got the job and the Tigers won two pennants in a row.

There was, however, life in the old boy yet. On a trip to Japan, in the company of such sluggers as Jimmy Foxx, Earl Averill and Lou Gehrig, Ruth won every individual championship. He led the American team in runs batted in, batting average, and of course, home runs. He made a lasting impression on the small, sport-loving and agile Japanese.

In the mid-Thirties, Ruth concentrated as much on golfing, deep-sea fishing and performing good works as he did on baseball. True, he was assistant manager of the Boston Braves for a time, and a coach with the Brooklyn Dodgers, but the jobs brought him little satisfaction. He recognized the fact that he was hired as a crowd-puller rather than for his coaching ability. In this, he never let the teams down.

In 1939, he participated in a sad event — Lou Gehrig Day at Yankee Stadium. Forced to stop playing because he had contracted a form of polio, Gehrig said good-bye to fans and the game in a touching ceremony. Few spectators could ignore the lumps in their throats when the Babe walked over to his former teammate, wished him luck, and hugged him.

In 1942, to help raise funds for Army-Navy Relief, Ruth batted against his old rival, Walter Johnson. To the delight of 60,000 fans, he poled one pitch into the third deck of the right-field stands and jogged around the bases in the old pigeon-toed manner.

In the last months of World War II, Ruth almost became a peace negotiator for the Allies. The plan was for a destroyer, painted white to anchor off the east coast of Japan. Ruth would then make a series of broadcasts to the Japanese, counting on his popularity there and on their love of baseball to convince them that they should surrender rather than risk annihilation. The Babe, eager to do his bit, was all for it. The plan, however, was turned down at a high government level as impractical.

In 1946, Ruth developed severe headaches and a sore throat. Ordered to the hospital by specialists, he lost weight at an alarming rate and it was clear he would not live long. No one ever received so many encouraging and hopeful letters from all over the world. Many of them were from men who, as kids, he had inspired with the magic therapy of his home-run bat. A few of them were given permission to wish him good luck personally.

A little more than a year after Babe Ruth Day — held in every park in organized baseball on March 8, 1947 — the Babe finally passed on.

In his obituary of the great man, Red Smith of the New York *Herald Tribune* wrote, "Somebody else will come along to hit sixty home runs, probably very soon. That won't make somebody else a second Babe Ruth. There won't ever be a second Babe Ruth. Never another like him."

The one memory of the Big Guy that most fans cherish was an incident which took place in 1932 when Ruth was thirty-seven and on the brink of being out of baseball.

The Yankees were playing the Cubs in the World Series, and few teams despised each other more. The Yankees charged that the Cubs were tightwads because of the way they had voted to divide up World Series' money (a former Yankee was being given less than they thought he deserved). The Cubs vented most of their spleen on the Babe, whom they called Grandpop, and Cub fans hooted at Babe and his wife whenever they appeared in public in Chicago.

In the third game of the Series, Ruth got his chance to hit the Cubs where it would do the most good. Subjected to considerable razzing by Wrigley Field spectators and the hostile Cub bench, Ruth faced Charley Root. The score was tied, 2–2, Earle Combs was on base and there was one out.

Root checked Combs and let fly. Ruth disdained the pitch, which was called a strike. He held up a finger, as though saying, "That's one." Root set himself and fired a second pitch. Two fingers were held up by the Babe. Then, in a gesture that will live as long as baseball, he pointed with his right hand to the far-off bleachers in center field.

The noise was deafening as Root's next pitch sped toward the plate. Ruth swung from his heels with every ounce of power he had, and the ball exploded from his bat and flew on a straight line to the spot in the bleachers he had pointed at.

As he jogged around the bases, Ruth doffed his cap to the stunned Cub team and then waved to the nearly silent crowd. It was the proudest, happiest moment of his life, he said later.

For the ten thousandth time, he had made millions of fans, and kids, proud and happy.

ERNEST HEMINGWAY
Writer

F ew writers of any age aroused as much comment and heated opinion as Ernest Hemingway. Unique artist, fiery personality and wily outdoorsman, Hemingway is sometimes called the spokesmen for "the lost generation." The lost generation is a term often taken to mean the pleasure-loving Americans, experimenters in the arts, who lived in Paris in the 1920's. But it is also taken to mean the entire generation of young people who came of age after World War I. Their main characteristic was a kind of disillusionment — but Hemingway, in writing about disillusioned people in *The Sun Also Rises*, is sometimes said to have been their inventor as well as their spokesmen; they adopted as their own the attitudes adopted by his characters.

In general, praise for his works has been high. Arthur Koestler called him the world's greatest living writer — at a time when Thomas Mann, George Bernard Shaw and William Faulkner were still active. (Tolstoi was Hemingway's favorite writer, while he thought William Faulkner had the most talent of any American, and his favorite American novel was Mark Twain's *Huckleberry Finn*.)

Some critics, admirers of his taut style and the skill he showed in creating deep meanings with simple words, consider him to have been the greatest writer of the Twentieth century. There is no doubt that he found ways to use the language which no writer had previously devised.

The English novelist, Ford Madox Ford, said of his style, "Hemingway's words strike you, each one, as if they were pebbles fetched fresh from a brook. They live and shine, each in its place. So, one of his pages has the effect of a brook-bottom into which you look down through the flowing water. The words form a tesselation [mosaic pattern], each in order beside the other."

John O'Hara, the brilliant author of *Appointment in Samarra*, went furthest of all. He called Hemingway "the outstanding author since the death of Shakespeare" — a claim that even Hemingway's most fervent fans might have trouble accepting. The extent of his influence is shown by the fact that his style is the most imitated of all American writers and also — if it is to his credit — the most frequently parodied.

Inevitably, such high praise has inspired other critics to attack his writing, and with it, the way he chose to live his life. Literary historian Van Wyck Brooks said Hemingway was a permanent adolescent in his concern for playing soldier. Another critic called his heroes blockheads. Still others have regarded Hemingway personally as a phony, actor and show-off. Gertrude Stein, the eccentric but wise authoress who befriended him in Paris and influenced his style but later broke with him, inferred that he was a coward — that the frank admiration he showed for courage in his works proved it. Another critic stated that there was an aura of false hair on his chest — also inferring that Hemingway was not as brave as he made himself out to be.

Whatever he was, Hemingway was not insensitive to criticism. The barbs hurt. He was unhappy when critics — great or small — found fault with his writing or voiced doubts about his valor.

Once, while fishing for marlin off Key West with his younger brother Leicester, Ernest brought up the subject of his personal courage. "Tell me, Baron," he said, "do I deliver or don't I?"

Leicester had seen Ernest struggle with and land huge fish, considered him a nerveless and dead shot with a variety of weapons, and knew him as a terror with his fists both in and out of the ring. He also remembered Ernest's stoic, even joking, acceptance of a score of wounds.

"Like nobody else," he assured his brother.

There is a powerful link between Hemingway's writing and his reactions to danger, discomfort and tragedy. Perhaps more than those of any other writer, his stories and novels reveal what he felt as he underwent many exciting and often unpleasant experiences. For him, the art of fiction consisted of arousing feelings of pain, tension, fear, passion, pride, pleasure and other emotions in the reader — just as they were aroused in Hemingway.

Unlike most writers, he looked for adventure of a violent sort, one of the reasons being to test his skills and courage under perilous circumstances. (Later, the skills and courage of his fiction heroes would be similarly tested.) He recorded events with unusual accuracy and clarity, and chose words which he hoped would convey his own emotions to the reader. It is a measure of his originality and honesty that he wanted to convey the emotions he actually felt — not those he was *supposed* to feel.

Despite his emphasis on courage as a prime virtue, however, his heroes were seldom triumphant in the usual sense; they were men who could accept defeat and tragedy without whimpering. It is as though Jake Barnes in *The Sun Also Rises*, Lieutenant Henry in *A Farewell to Arms* and the bullfighter in *The Undefeated* were somehow purified by the disasters that engulfed them. Few of his heroes do not bear terrible wounds.

Writing, though Hemingway sweated over it, gave him great delight. In 1922, he remarked to a friend, "My writing is nothing. My boxing is everything." But later, when his writing found an audience, he said, "Nothing is worth anything but the truth as you know it, feel it and create it in fiction."

While living in the Florida Keys and working on *A Farewell to Arms* (which many think to be the best war novel by an American), he was beset by troubles and tragedy, including the death of his father by suicide. Ernest had great affection for the bearded, brawny Dr. Hemingway, and he was shocked by his father's act. But so absorbed was he in developing the personalities of his American lieutenant and English nurse for the novel, that he could put the tragic event out of his mind.

"Finding you were able to make something up," he explained later, "to create truly enough so that it made you happy to read it; and to do this every day you worked was something that gave a greater pleasure than any I had ever known. Beside it, nothing else mattered." It was 1926 and he was twenty-seven at the time.

He wrote not only to please himself or to shock the reader

into examining his own feelings, however. For Hemingway, oddly enough, writing was a kind of medicine. By writing about what bothered him, he purged himself of unpleasant memories and despondent thoughts. In the 1930's, he was asked who his psychoanalyst was. The extremely self-reliant adventurer (who did not much believe in analysis by strangers) laughingly replied that it was his typewriter. Since he also maintained that he killed animals to keep from killing himself, he might have added, "And my rifle."

He was a well-rounded man, a quick learner, filled with a zest for living, and occupied by many enthusiasms. He was a seeker of wars, a hunter of big game, a lover of bull-fighting and cockfighting, a tireless fisherman, an arbiter of good food and drink, and an expert on military tactics. For the most part, his favorite companions were not literary people but more physical types — prizefighters, bicycle racers, commercial fishermen, toreros. He was fond of movie stars (Gary Cooper, Ingrid Bergman, Marlene Dietrich), Basques, West Point generals, the Duke and Duchess of Windsor, and convicts who escaped from Devil's Island. His deepest admiration was for persons who showed great skill in their specialties, who followed their own strict codes of behavior and who lived with danger as a matter of course.

Hemingway, who faced danger as a matter of choice, relished it at its most critical. Once, at a fiesta in Spain, he rescued Donald Ogden Stewart from the horns of a bull. He once broke up a dog fight by seizing one of the dogs (a large collie) and heaving him over a high wall. And he beat up a prizefighter who had almost killed a lighter boxer.

Perhaps the most cherished compliment Hemingway ever received came, not from a critic or colleague, but from a boxer. It was given in 1920 when Hemingway was a barrel-chested, iron-calved, open-faced young journalist on his way to feverish Paris to learn to write. While aboard the French liner *Leopoldina,* he fought several rounds with a Salt Lake City middleweight named Henry Cuddy, who had bouts scheduled in Europe.

"You're good," commented Cuddy after the panting pair embraced at the end of the final round. "You ought to turn pro." Ernest flashed his beacon smile. His bride, who had acted as his second and chief rooter, echoed his pleasure.

Though he thought what he had to say was more important than a professional ring career, Ernest had scores of other boxing adventures. During a sojourn in Northern Bimini, an island in the Caribbean, he was enjoying remarkable luck with his fishing — developing a technique of landing fish quickly, before marauding sharks could rip them to pieces. On an evening when he returned to the dock empty-handed, however, he was confronted by a large man who began to berate him as a phony.

Unable to calm the stranger down, and made angry by further insults, Ernest climbed onto the dock and threw a few punches. In a bareknuckle, barefoot fight in bad light, he finally knocked the man out. His opponent, he learned the next day, was not Jack Dempsey or Gene Tunney (as the Hemingway legend would seem to demand) but an important magazine publisher. The publisher apologized for doubting Hemingway's courage, and that ended the matter, except that Hemingway was in some anguish from having ripped the toenails off two toes in defense of his reputation.

Not long after the publication of his book of short stories, *Winner Take Nothing,* Hemingway boxed several rounds with the former British heavyweight champion, Tom Heeney, on a deserted beach at Northern Bimini. The bout, which was going about even, came to an end when Ernest noticed a crowd of curious onlookers standing on a path above the beach. Rather than continue the free show, the formidable pair slipped off their gloves and went swimming.

Around this time, he offered $200 to any native of the island who could stay four rounds with him. Several tried it, but none won the $200. At Key West, Hemingway changed his role of spectator to that of participant at the end of one suspicious bout. He leapt into the ring and persuaded the winner to insist to the referee that he had fouled his "unconscious" opponent and deserved to lose the fight. The decision was reversed, and those involved in the fix lost their bets while Hemingway gained a horde of local admirers and friends.

Boxing was a major interest throughout Hemingway's life, perhaps because he thought it as direct a test as could be found for a man's character. He sparred with his friends, as relaxation and to work off excess energy. As his reputation as a fighter increased, he found himself repeatedly challenged, in bars and other places, by strangers who had doubts about his ability or willingness to return a punch. Like many "tough-guy" screen actors similarly challenged, he was happy to oblige, always giving a good account of himself in these impromptu bouts.

One might suppose, from his obsession with boxing, that one or both parents had encouraged him in this activity — in the way Dempsey's hard-working mother hoped he would be another John L. Sullivan. The exact opposite is true. Ernest's father, Dr. Clarence Hemingway, a medical examiner for insurance companies and an obstetrician, wanted his son to become a doctor. Dr. Hemingway was a kindly, retiring man with a horror of fighting — even when it was justified. As a youth, while in the presence of his grandmother, he had been handed a fearful beating by a larger boy. His grandmother, as a matter of principle, had refused to let him hit the bully back.

While Dr. Hemingway did like shooting, hunting and fishing, his wife Grace abhorred violence of any kind. A pianist and talented singer who gave up a career to marry, Grace wanted her son to become a singer or instrumentalist. At her wish, Ernest for many years practiced the cello in a large music room in the Hemingway home in Oak Park, Illinois, a middle-class suburb of Chicago. He was even taken out of school for a while so that he could devote more time to mastering the difficult instrument.

Ernest did not rebel about practice, but his mind wandered as he bowed the standard compositions. He once said that the flights of imagination his mind engaged in while he practiced convinced him that he had a talent for storytelling. While not a tuneful singer, he upheld family tradition by singing in the church choir. Discipline in the Hemingway home was of a Victorian sort: when Ernest used profanity, his mouth was washed out with soap.

Sensitive and wise beyond his years, Hemingway had an unusual childhood, with pleasure and pain equally mixed, and his talent for being original asserting itself early. He was born on July 21, 1899, the second child and first son in the family. Eventually it was to consist of three more girls and a second son, Leicester.

Because Dr. Hemingway approved of shooting (if it was for food), had an impressive gun collection, and was a keen-eyed wing shot, Ernest came to know and respect firearms early. In fact, Hemingway boys and girls alike had regular Sunday target practice, learning to love the pungent smell of gunpowder.

The Hemingways spent summers at a cottage they owned on Lake Walloon in Northern Michigan. There Ernest, an alert listener, picked up fishing and hunting lore from his father and uncles. He was enchanted with the primitive nature of the deep forest and the quiet lake, spending some of the happiest days of his life fishing and hunting with his father. He also developed muscles and strong lungs by pitching hay and making deep dives in the lake. Walking barefoot on pine needles was more to his liking than playing tunes on the cello.

During these summers he was also exposed to drama and tragedy that were to figure in his later stories. He learned about a brutal side of life when he accompanied his father to the homes of the Ojibway Indians who needed medical attention, and when he made other excursions into the strange world of grown-ups. His reactions to these adventures in Michigan were recorded in a short story collection called *In Our Time*. A character named Nick Adams is introduced to anguish, fear, fright and disappointment — just as his creator had been. In a story called "The Doctor and the Doctor's Wife," Hemingway wrote about his father's refusal to fight when a fight was justified, and the bond that existed between him and his father in spite of this. In "Indian Camp," he tells about an operation his father performed on a squaw and the pride Dr. Hemingway felt in his work under primitive conditions.

His father's medical skill came in handy once when Ernest, running to do an errand for his mother, fell down with a stick in his hand. The point went deep into his throat, and he barely made the trip back to the cottage before he fainted from loss of blood. His father patched him up, but the wound gave him trouble from time to time after that, even as an adult. He learned a lesson from the experience.

"When you're in pain," his father told him, "whistle." It was a piece of advice Ernest never forgot. It became, indeed, a code of behavior for the characters he created; those he admired most accepted pain without a whimper.

In high school in Oak Park, Ernest showed his versatility by playing right guard on a championship football team, writing for the school paper and hoaxing the student body by inventing a rifle club whose fantastic shooting scores he dutifully reported whenever space needed to be filled. To please his mother, he played cello in the school orchestra.

When a bully beat him up while he was paying a visit to an uncle in southern Illinois, Ernest's reaction was vastly different from his father's. He sped to Chicago to take boxing lessons, and the first lesson was a hard one. Urged to spar with Young A'Hearn, a hard-hitting pro middleweight, Ernest accepted and found himself flat on his back with a broken nose. It was not too great a surprise.

"The minute we exchanged looks, I knew he was going to tag me one," he told a friend afterward.

"Were you scared?"

Ernest grinned and nodded. "Bet your life I was scared."

"Why did you go in there with him?"

"I wasn't *that* scared."

Instead of quitting, as many of A'Hearn's victims did, Ernest persisted and became adept at the sport. He even boldly turned his mother's music room into a boxing gym. There, with his younger sister Sunny acting as second, sentinel and timekeeper, he engaged in afternoon bouts with his school chums. If his parents knew about the odd rituals in the music room, they never mentioned the fact to Ernest — even when he showed up at supper one night with an eye damaged by the metal tip of a flying glove lace.

When America entered World War I in 1917, Ernest, about to graduate from high school, burned with eagerness to become part of it. He was extremely conscious of the war — as the slogans he was bombarded with intended that he should be — as a crusade for democracy. His parents, however, forbade him to join the Army. They wanted him to attend Oberlin College in Ohio.

A compromise was reached when Ernest, who thought he would like to be a newspaperman, went to work on the Kansas City *Star*. He did police reporting, interviewed owners of lost dogs, and covered fires. An enthusiastic legman, he did such a thorough job of reporting one fire that his best suit burned off from contact with the flames. He was crestfallen when the editor refused to let him charge the paper for it.

During Ernest's absence, his father relented about letting him join the Army. Ernest tried to enlist, but was turned down because of his eyesight. (Though he had realized that his eyes were not good, he stubbornly refused to wear glasses regularly until he was thirty years old.)

Fearful of missing the war completely, in February, 1918, he jumped at the chance of joining the American Red Cross Field Service. Assigned to the Italian theatre, Ernest sailed for Europe, filled with ideals and good-fellowship. He got his first look at Paris — later to be his favorite city — while it was being shelled by the Germans, and finally arrived at Fossalte di Piave, in Italy, where lively combat was going on.

During the early morning hours of July 9th, the most dramatic event of his life occurred. An Austrian trench-mortar bomb exploded in the midst of several Italian soldiers. Two men were killed immediately, one had his legs blown off. Ernest himself was knocked unconscious.

"I died then," he told a friend later. "I felt my soul or something coming right out of my body, like you'd pull a silk handkerchief out of a pocket by one corner. It flew around and then came back and went in again and I wasn't dead anymore."

Despite the shock of the explosion and having received over 230 pieces of steel rods in his legs, Ernest picked up the man who was still alive and started to carry him to an aid station in the rear. Searchlights caught him in their beams, and he was hit twice more in the legs by machine-gun fire. "My legs were a mess," Hemingway later wrote his family, showing a gift for understatement.

After reaching the aid station, he laid down his burden and collapsed. The soldier was found to be dead. Then Hemingway spent three months in hospitals, getting the shrapnel fragments removed from his legs. After his right knee and right foot were operated on, he had to learn to walk all over again. (Like his main character in *Across the River and Into the Trees*, Ernest felt a kinship with the Italian earth because he had lost a kneecap defending it. An Italian surgeon fixed him up with an aluminum kneecap.)

At a field hospital outside Milan, Ernest had an idyllic love affair with an American nurse. After her transfer to other hospitals in Italy, they continued to correspond, Ernest urging her to marry him. But she refused, and for a while he was quite despondent. Later she would become the model for Catherine Barkley, the tragic heroine of *A Farewell to Arms*. In other works, Ernest would write about the shattering effect his wound had on him — its disillusioning him about the "glory" of war and making him fear the night. Like his wounded hero Jake Barnes, he could not sleep without a light in his room for a long time afterward.

Returning home, covered with Italy's highest decorations, he found himself a hero — a severely wounded veteran who had seen the war at firsthand. He became filled with a kind of restlessness, however, and was glad to be able to escape memories of war, that summer, by visiting the cool, peaceful Michigan woods. He tried his hand at fiction, acquiring a fistful of rejection slips, but managed to get his name into print by writing articles for the Toronto *Star,* whose editor considered him a good craftsman.

After an unsatisfying fling at editing a small magazine in Chicago — where he met Sherwood Anderson, author of *Winesburg, Ohio,* and other writers — Ernest confronted his family with two surprises. The first was marrying a St. Louis girl — Hadley Richardson — whom he had met in Chicago. The second was his firm decision to abandon America and live and write in Europe.

As Ernest had desperately wished, he was appointed European correspondent for the Toronto *Star.* This would give him a chance to earn a living and learn his trade on the continent he loved (perhaps because, unlike America, it had been severely wounded).

Sherwood Anderson gave him letters of introduction to writers in Paris, and Ernest and Hadley immediately became part of the expatriate American colony inhabiting the legendary Left Bank. Some members of the colony — writers, artists, dancers, poets, sculptors — had gone there to take advantage of the section's low prices, some reveled in the air of creative freedom that prevailed, and some were hangers-on, happy to live a Bohemian life and bask in the creative achievements of the more industrious and talented. Imbued with a spirit of desperate fun, the night throbbing with the fiery tempo of jazz bands, Paris was a kind of last frontier for these expatriates. They rejected America as being too industrialized, too in love with material possessions, too dull.

Ford Madox Ford says of them: "Young America, from

the limitless prairies, leapt, released, on Paris. They stampeded with the madness of colts when you let down the slip-rails between dried pasture and green. The noise of their advancing drowned out all sounds . . . their perpetual motion made you dizzy."

Expatriate Hemingway had long talks about life and writing with Ford, John Dos Passos and James Joyce. He discussed writing techniques with Gertrude Stein and the poet Ezra Pound, both of whom influenced him greatly, and tried to teach Pound how to box. "He leads with his chin and has the grace of a crawfish," Ernest told a friend, but he admired Pound for risking his dignity.

"Begin over again and concentrate," was Miss Stein's terse advice when Ernest showed her his writing. He found it good advice.

Though he partied and drank with the expatriates and nearly got killed by shards of glass from a falling skylight, Ernest was too busy to become the complete Bohemian. For the *Star,* he covered the European economic conference in Genoa, and met such colorful personalities as Lloyd George, Mussolini and Clemenceau. When he had free time, he hiked in the forests of Compiègne and Chantilly, fished in the Rhone Valley, skied in the Alps, and lived with a group of bullfighters in Spain.

The *Star* sent him to Constantinople to cover the conflict between Turkey and Greece, and he followed the armies west through Thrace. "Here is where I really learned about war," he said, deeply impressed by the agony of refugees helplessly caught up in it. Like his Michigan adventures, these experiences inspired short stories, some of which appeared in *Men Without Women* and *In Our Time.*

At the end of 1922, he went to Lausanne, Switzerland, for the peace conference between Greece and Turkey.

Meeting Hadley there, he received the bad news that a suitcase full of stories he had written had been stolen from her
while she was on the train. The suitcase could not be recovered.

Undaunted, Ernest started writing anew, helped by advice
from Gertrude Stein and Ezra Pound, and influenced by
what he had seen of war and what he saw on the Left Bank.
Oddly enough, from 1919 to 1927, he sent dozens of stories
to American magazines without being able to sell one —
until *The Atlantic Monthly* published "Fifty Grand," a
story about a prizefighter who suffered terrible pain but
refused to go down. European magazines bought several
Hemingway stories, however, and in 1925 his first significant short-story collection, *In Our Time,* was published in
New York. It was a failure, except that some of the bluntly
worded tales shocked the residents of Oak Park.

It took only a week in 1926 to write his first novel, *Tor-
rents of Spring,* a parody on Sherwood Anderson's works.
This, too, was a failure. But encouraged by F. Scott Fitzgerald, Ernest threw himself into finishing his next novel.
Fitzgerald, who made it a special point to visit Hemingway
while he was in Paris, was one of the first to note Hemingway's great talent, and the two became fast friends.

The Sun Also Rises, published in the same year, was an
immediate success. It is a masterful account of the despair
underlying the devil-may-care attitudes of foreigners in
Paris, the novel's characters all seeking, in the pleasantest
way possible, their own self-destruction. Jake Barnes, con-
signed to a living death, speaks for Hemingway and rejects
civilization, society and phony sentimentality. The heroine,
Lady Brett, is completely unmoral.

Without precisely meaning to, Hemingway gave voice to
feelings the young generation of the time had been unable

to find expressed. They read the book and began to talk the way Hemingway characters talked; they acted disenchanted in the way he described.

Suddenly beseiged by magazine editors for stories, he devoted full time to fiction except for skiing, hunting and fishing, finding a kind of poetry in all three activities. In 1927, *Men Without Women* was published. This book of short stories contains "The Killers" and "The Undefeated." The first is about a pair of murderers calmly stalking their victim, but below the surface of the action is Hemingway's condemnation of a society that would allow murder to be committed (a characteristic of the Twenties) without trying to stop it. The second is about an aging bullfighter, and re-veals Hemingway's belief that to be killed while courting danger is a kind of triumph. They are considered to be among the best short stories ever written.

Returning to see his family in America the following year, he settled finally in Key West, became an addict of big-game fishing, and finished *A Farewell to Arms*. This novel is based partly on his experiences in combat in Italy in 1918 and expresses more of the disillusionment that had been building in him about a society that glorified war.

It was published just before the Stock Market crash of 1929 — the shocking event that rang down the curtain on the giddier features of the Twenties. Like *The Sun Also Rises*, it struck a deep chord of understanding in Americans and established Hemingway, at thirty, as a novelist and storyteller of the first rank.

In the Thirties, Hemingway was a big-game hunter but found time to produce scores of magazine articles, a book of short stories — *Winner Take Nothing* — a book about hunting in Africa, *To Have and Have Not* (in which his hero is a former rumrunner), and *Death in the Afternoon*.

The last is considered to be the best book on bullfighting in any language.

Toward the end of the decade, he became deeply involved in the Spanish Civil War, an event that inspired the writing of his best-known book, *For Whom the Bell Tolls.*

Hemingway was called a war correspondent in World War II, but he was a good deal more than that: he headed his own group of French Underground fighters against the Germans, and often found himself far in advance of the Allied front lines. Called "Papa" by most soldiers, he was considered by many the bravest man they had ever seen.

Cuba became his home after the war, and he lived in a house with thirty cats ("A cat has absolute emotional honesty," he told his brother) and continued to hunt for big fish and write.

In 1953, he received the Pulitzer prize for *The Old Man and the Sea.* The following year he received literature's highest award — the Nobel prize — partly for that novel and partly for "his powerful and style-forming mastery of the art of modern narration."

In February, 1961, sick and depressed and disenchanted with Cuba, Hemingway was making his home in Ketcham, Idaho. Having lived a dozen more lives than most people and having set down his impressions of those lives as honestly and vigorously as he knew how, he shot himself early one morning with his favorite shotgun. His books and stories are the best kind of epitaph.

ADMIRAL RICHARD E. BYRD
Polar Explorer

From the time of the ancient Greeks, as terrifying as the
Arctic has seemed — with its wide expanses of hostile ice,
its treacherous gales and benumbing cold — this alien area
has held an irresistible enchantment for many. For cen-
turies, it existed as a blank, uncharted spot on maps, with
few of its mysterious characteristics known.

In summer, daylight lasts for six months; in winter, it is
dismal and dark and there is no hope of seeing the sun.
Strange animals dwell in its reaches — the blubbery nar-
whal, tusked walruses, spouting whales — and strange people, whose main effort is merely to survive.

For 2,500 years, men have tried to extend the limits of
their knowledge about the Arctic. It has been attacked
by dog sled, dragon boat, square-rigger, icebreaker, bal-
loon, submarine, dirigible and plane. In the fifteenth cen-

tury, the English and Dutch raced to find a Northwest Passage to India. Peter the Great of Russia sent out an expedition to see if America and Asia were linked. Later, commercial enterprises were launched, with hunters and trappers advancing north, winning their way against scurvy, snow blindness, frozen limbs and the awesome, lonely barrenness of the top of the world.

In no area of the globe have men made progress so slowly and with as much suffering. The pole itself — the earth's northern axis where all lines of longitude meet and to which the compass needle magically seems to point — had not been reached by the end of the 19th century.

It was the unflagging ambition of curly-haired young Dick Byrd, son of a scholarly, bespectacled Virginia lawyer, to discover the North Pole. Reading about it had set his imagination aflame — especially the story of Elisha Kent Kane, an American doctor and explorer. In 1850, Kane was a member of the Grinnell Expedition which searched for Sir John Franklin, a British explorer who had mysteriously vanished in the Arctic. Three years later, head of his own expedition, Kane reached the northernmost point yet attained by man.

Byrd showed, at an early age, the valor and self-reliance characteristic of explorers. Small for his age but wiry, he never backed down from fights. He wandered afar and late, despite parental scoldings, through the rugged Blue Ridge Mountains with his dog Judy. The first time he sailed a boat he sailed it across a bay near his home in Winchester — in the face of a howling squall. When not off on his solitary adventures, he built up his body by boxing, swimming, riding horseback and running long distances.

His mother, father and two brothers were shocked when, at the age of thirteen, Dick insisted on going to the Philippines. His uncle Adam Carson, who was a provincial judge there, had invited him to pay a visit. Dick's parents quite naturally refused him permission. Not only did the distance seem fantastically far in 1902, but conditions were far from peaceful. A rebellion had broken out against the Americans, who were governing the island after the war against Spain. Cases of deadly cholera had broken out. But Dick was a persistent pleader, and finally his parents reluctantly gave him permission to go.

Dick nearly got his fill of adventure. Within the year he had calmed hysterical passengers on his ship during a typhoon and had almost been killed by bolo-wielding guerrillas when he fell into a river ambush. He finally was sent home when cholera struck down soldiers on all sides of him during an epidemic. He went by way of Saigon, Singapore, Calcutta and Gibraltar. By 1903 — the year the Wright Brothers flew their rickety plane 120 feet at Kitty Hawk — Dick was a world traveler.

Lucky to have returned with a whole skin after his trip to the Philippines, he became known as "Hard Luck Byrd" because of his physical problems during the next few years. He left Virginia Military Institute to study law at the University of Virginia, and forsook law to attend Annapolis.

"I want to explore," he told his father earnestly, "and most explorers are naval men." But he very nearly failed to graduate, despite being brilliant in geography, navigation, applied physics and math — the ABC's of the explorer.

As a Navy quarterback he made a long broken-field run against Princeton, and when he tried to rise from the pile-up after scoring, he found that his foot was broken in three places. On a training cruise his class made, he came down with typhoid and was hospitalized in England. It was here, in 1908, that he learned of Admiral Peary's discovery of the North Pole. He despaired for several days, then shrugged off his disappointment, assuming — and rightly — that there would be other firsts for him. Characteristically, because he wanted to get in shape for football, he did push-ups on the ward floor after lights were out.

Back at Annapolis, his most tragic accident occurred. As captain of the gym team, he practiced on the flying rings, perfecting a spectacular stunt which he hoped would give Navy a victory over Yale. It was a double dislocate — something like a pair of backward somersaults done high in the air. On the second one, he was to bring his legs outside the rings, letting go and catching them again. The timing was extremely critical.

He swung up very high, completed the first movement — and then, after letting go the rings and whirling around, failed to seize them. The crowd gasped as he plummeted to the floor below and hit with a sickening thud. His right ankle was smashed.

Dreams of glory set aside, Byrd boned up on his studies while in the hospital. Painful though his ankle was, he stubbornly refused — as he was advised — to wait another year before graduating. The Norwegian explorer, Roald Amundsen, had discovered the South Pole, and Byrd was impatient to launch some kind of exploration of his own.

Unfortunately, even though he managed to graduate, he had to wait. At first the waiting was not too unpleasant. There was unrest in the Caribbean in 1912, as well as in Europe, and Byrd, though he limped when he walked, served with distinction in several skirmishes. He was on the battleship that helped capture Veracruz, Mexico, held by the Mexican dictator Huerta, took part in assaults against rebels in Haiti and Santo Domingo, and on two occasions leapt overboard to save shipmates from drowning.

Then, to his disgust, because of his weak ankle he was

taken off his battlewagon and assigned to "social duty" aboard the yacht of the Secretary of the Navy, in the Potomac. The only exciting thing that happened to Hard Luck Byrd at this time was taking his first airplane ride. To cheer him up, a young pilot drove him to the dock, showed him the flimsy craft with its open fuselage, wooden wings and wire struts, helped him stuff cotton in his ears and invited his nautical friend to hop aboard.

Byrd, despite his worry that the craft might vibrate to pieces as the pontoon smacked against the waves and shivered and wheezed as it became airborne, had never been so thrilled in his life. Cold and wet, he peered down to see hangars, boats and houses sink away as the plane labored to climb higher and higher. By the time it had shuddered down to a bumpy landing on the waves, Byrd foresaw its value as the perfect device for exploring uncharted areas. No longer would the explorer have to trek painfully and slowly along the ground, able to see only a few miles on either side. He could fly above obstacles such as rivers, mountains and ice, covering vast distances in a short span of time.

His mind was made up. He would be an explorer by air. The first step was to cease being a tea-party ensign and get transferred to what was then the most primitive branch of service — Naval Aviation.

He discussed his decision with his bride, Marie Barton, with whom he had grown up in Winchester. Marie was overjoyed that he had found precisely what he wanted to do. Byrd's father, however, had little faith in heavier-than-air craft. He thought, as many did, that every flier sooner or later crashed in flames. Dirigibles were considered much safer; one could see what was holding them up.

Unfortunately, Ensign Byrd had reckoned without practical Navy doctors. He was refused both a transfer and a promotion — because of his weak ankle. One year before the United States entered World War I, Byrd made a drastic decision: he resigned from the Navy. Sadly he wrote in his diary: "Career ended. No chance of coming back. Trained for a seafaring profession; temperamentally unsuited for business. A fizzle."

But when unrestricted submarine warfare by the Germans brought an angry America into war, Byrd found himself back in the Navy, though he suffered through a series of dull desk jobs. The lack of action when so much that was exciting was taking place drove him to despair and his health declined.

Finally the head of the district medical board called him in. "Byrd," said the doctor, "you've been working too hard. We think you ought to go on a long sick leave."

"It's this desk work," Byrd said, aware that he looked thin and drawn. "I'd get better quick if you'd let me transfer to Naval Aviation." His eyes pleaded with the doctor.

"But you're in terrible shape. And," the doctor added, not without sympathy, "what about that weak ankle?" He recalled that standing long watches aboard ship had always been an ordeal for Byrd.

"All I ask," argued Byrd, "is that you put off your decision for a month. Let me go to Pensacola and fly. You don't fly with your legs."

In peacetime, Byrd's plea would have been flatly declined, but now the country had need of brave, determined young men, regardless of their physical imperfections.

"You have one month," said the doctor. "Go to flying school — but then you'll have to take a thorough physical. And you'd better pass it."

After a grinning salute, Byrd hurtled out of the office, the happiest ensign in the Navy.

Valise in hand, Dick was greeted at Pensacola, Florida,

by a sputtering aircraft high over the water which suddenly dove down in the tight spiral of a tailspin. As mechanics stopped their work, looked up and shouted in alarm and a rescue boat headed for the middle of the bay, the plane, whistling as it turned, smacked hard into the water, sending up an explosion of spray.

"How often does this happen?" Byrd asked a mechanic.

"Oh, at least once a day," the mechanic replied. "That's not counting collisions in the air. These fellows are pretty green." Satisfied that he had given the new student something to think about, the mechanic returned to his engine.

Undaunted by the dangers he faced in the wobbly, uncertain planes, Byrd flung himself into aviation with his usual zeal. He relived the thrill of his first flight, took apart and put together engines, and soaked up aerial knowledge like a sponge. After only six hours as a student flier he was ready to solo. He enjoyed the ride immensely until it came time for him to land. Then, to his dismay, his plane slammed down on the water so hard that it bounced back into the air, where it shuddered uncertainly and drove on. For an hour and a half the desperate Byrd tried landings. Finally he brought the plane down without bouncing it, and proudly taxied through choppy water to the concrete ramp.

Byrd got healthier day by day, passed his physical easily, and was appointed an instructor. In his spare time he studied night flying — a dangerous branch of aviation — and invented a bubble sextant, an instrument that allowed a navigator to determine the sun's elevation without seeing the horizon. As early as 1918 — perhaps because he regretted not being able to fight on the Western Front — he argued with superiors that he should be allowed to fly over the North Pole. Defeated in this, he contended that he should be allowed to fly the Atlantic in a hydroplane.

"It would give the men's morale a boost," he claimed,

"and it would show the world what Naval aviation can do."

Nor did Byrd lose faith in the airplane when, just after taking off, a nervous student pilot zoomed down on his rising craft. The wings of the two planes tangled, and out of control, they spanked into the water. Luckily, Byrd and the other pilot were found to suffer from nothing but bruises, though both planes were demolished.

The eminent Admiral Peary backed Byrd's plan to fly the Atlantic, and Byrd hopped a train to Washington, D. C., expecting to receive orders empowering him to make preparations for the flight. He planned to use a flying boat with three motors, taking a crew of five. But to his intense chagrin, the orders he received dispatched him to Halifax, in Newfoundland, where he was to take charge of the Naval Air Station. Planes based there were to keep the shipping lanes clear of submarines. German undersea boats were disappointingly scarce, however, and Byrd busied himself by supervising parachute-jumping — a novel and risky art — inventing a handy instrument for pilots called a driftmeter and solving the navigation problems he might encounter if he should one day be allowed to fly the Atlantic.

When the war ended, the Navy decided to test the new-found skill of its pilots and its improved machines by having three of them fly from Trepassey, in Newfoundland, to the Azores, and thence to Portugal. Unfortunately for Byrd, whom many considered the best navigator in the Navy, personnel having had foreign duty (including duty in Canada) were ineligible for the flight. For reasons of overwork or despair, Byrd fell prey to the vicious flu bug which was attacking thousands — and recovered only when he was told that he could take charge of navigating the planes up to Trepassey. Once he had gotten them there, he hoped that he would be allowed to sneak off on one of them unnoticed.

But special orders arrived directing Byrd not to make the flight. He aided in the planes' departure and waved them off. Only one of the three craft reached the Azores; the other two crashed in the Atlantic. Luckily, all crew members were saved.

As a kind of sop to his feelings, Byrd was assigned to the C-5, a dirigible stationed in St. John's, Newfoundland. Rumor had it that the airship might make an attempt at crossing the Atlantic, but a strong wind blew it sky-high from its moorings when no one was aboard, and another dream was shattered.

Returning to Washington, Byrd suggested that he fly alone from Newfoundland to England, but was shunted off instead to another dirigible — this time the ZR-2. This craft, built in England and purchased by the United States Navy, was about to fly from Howden, England, to Long Island. Byrd hastened to London, then took a train to Howden, arriving too late to be a passenger on the ZR-2's trial run. He was fortunate to be late. The dirigible blew up in midair and fell in the Humber River. Only five of fifty aboard survived.

This was not Byrd's last experience with dirigibles. In January, 1924, as a reward for his having done a superb job of setting up naval air stations around the country, the Navy assigned him to the *Shenandoah*. President Coolidge had approved a flight by the dirigible over the North Pole, and Byrd was to plan the flight and assist in the navigation. But a few days before its scheduled departure, a violent storm flung the airship from its mooring mast and gave it a severe pounding and President Coolidge called off the flight.

Then flying over the Pole, for Byrd at least, took on the aspects of a race. Roald Amundsen was in the United States, assembling funds to enable him and his crew to be the first men to perform this feat. In a sense, it was airplane versus

73

dirigible, for Amundsen planned to fly in the Italian-made dirigible *Norge*, while Byrd placed his faith in more easily maneuverable heavier-than-air craft.

He was determined to beat Amundsen, and previous frustrations now guided his thinking. No longer relying on the Navy for support, he began making ready his own expedition. Then he was confronted, as most explorers are, with the unpleasant job of asking wealthy people to support the enterprise. The amount required, he soon came to realize, was staggering. Some money was raised, mainly from Edsel Ford — Henry's son — and John D. Rockefeller, Jr. But it was not enough to pay for all essentials — one of those essentials being an airplane.

After nearly losing hope, Byrd was finally persuaded to join forces with Commander Donald B. MacMillan, who was planning a nautical expedition to the western section of Greenland. If Byrd would lend his navigational skills to the MacMillan party, the Navy would turn over to him an amphibian plane. Not overjoyed that MacMillan would have charge of the expedition, Byrd saw the advantages of cooperating. MacMillan had Navy backing and a ship which would transport Byrd's plane to a northern base. From there he planned to fly over the pole.

Byrd was thirty-seven years old when, in June, 1925, he and his crew started out with MacMillan's group on the sturdy *Peary*, which left from Maine and battered and sloshed its way through ice floes and past mountainous icebergs until it reached Etah, in western Greenland. This was the tiny settlement Byrd had chosen for his base of operations. Fighting sub-zero cold and winds of gale force, he and his men built a runway over rocks and ice under the light of a faint, always visible, sun.

Byrd found, though, that he had overestimated the length

of the Arctic summer; not enough good flying weather remained for the trip to the pole. Once again his North Pole flight would have to be postponed. He also concluded, after weighing the many problems involved, that the takeoff point would have to be much farther north than Etah. He made use of the time he had by testing the plane under Arctic conditions and making the first flight across the Greenland icecap, a mile-high plateau of solid ice. The most fortunate aspect of the expedition was Byrd's getting to know Floyd Bennett, a flier as good as Byrd, a brilliant mechanic, and like Byrd, a man completely without fear.

Back in America, Byrd began the tedious task of raising more funds. It was easier this time, since his expedition had made him better known and many Americans were eager to see him beat Amundsen. The Norwegian explorer's dirigible was nearly ready for the flight.

Nevertheless, Byrd was $20,000 in debt when his ship, the *Chantier*, left New York on April 25, 1926. A three-engine single-wing plane, the *Josephine Ford* (named for Edsel's daughter), was lashed to her deck. If his flight were successful, he hoped to earn enough to pay his debts by giving lectures; if not. . . .

On reaching Kings Bay in Spitsbergen, lying about midway between the North Cape of Norway and the North Pole, Byrd was somewhat dismayed to find Amundsen's crew already set up there, waiting the arrival of the *Norge*. A second blow was that he would be unable to use the small dock at the Kings Bay coaling station to unload his aircraft. A Norwegian gunboat, having recently escaped being crushed by the relentless ice, was tied up there. The captain, fearful of his ship's safety, refused to cast off. He gave Byrd — whom he considered an amateur in fighting against jagged, tumbling masses of ice — a stern warning to leave, lest his own ship be crushed.

But Byrd had not come this far to turn back. He gave the order to lower four whaleboats from the *Chantier* and to lash them together. Planks were placed over them, forming a crude raft. Onto this the plane would be lowered. The temperature was 15 below.

In the next few hours, Byrd's expedition nearly came to an end several times. Just as the plane was about to be lowered, a sudden snow squall, rising swiftly, snapped the lines holding its wings. Only quick work by Byrd and the crew, all tugging fiercely at the ropes, kept the plane from smashing into the superstructure of the ship. After the squall had dissipated and the plane had been made secure to the raft, the contrivance was towed to shore by oarsmen in another whaleboat. Halfway there, a huge iceberg, carried by the current, threatened to collide with it. Byrd hastily sent for dynamite which crewmen lodged in the iceberg. The dynamite, exploding with a muffled rumble, split the iceberg into large, jagged shards which dispersed in the choppy water.

After cheering the efforts of Byrd's crew to get the plane to shore, the Norwegians lent a hand and it was hoisted onto a projecting shelf of ice. The next task — hauling the plane a mile up hill to the only takeoff site available — seemed easy by comparison.

The takeoff itself, however, presented unusual problems. For the first time, a plane of this size would be attempting a downhill, rather than level, run. It would also be the first time a plane would try a takeoff on skis. But the main difficulty was the roughness of the runway. Byrd's determined crew worked eighteen hours a day to smooth it sufficiently for the downhill glide, hacking at ridges of ice with axes and hatchets, and stamping down the jagged surface with freezing feet.

Finally the strip was considered ready. Byrd and Bennett climbed into the *Josephine Ford* and set its sluggish motors to throbbing in the Arctic air. When the motors were thoroughly warmed up, down the hill the craft lumbered, watched tensely by Americans and Norwegians alike. The plane struggled to rise off the snow, failed and crashed with a thud into a snowbank at the end of the runway.

"Too much weight, not enough speed," was Byrd's laconic comment when he found the only serious damage was a broken ski.

"The runway has got to be made smoother," Bennett said

Despite some frostbitten fingers, the crew repaired the damaged ski and the plane was hauled back up the hill. The runway was smoothed out flatter. Excess weight was tossed off the plane. But again it failed to rise off the snow.

A third attempt, a third failure — and Byrd was more discouraged than he had ever been. The skis were now damaged beyond repair. Both he and Bennett had been averaging only a few hours sleep each night.

"I guess," Byrd remarked to him sadly, "a plane can't do the job. Amundsen has the right idea."

Then two crewmen, almost as eager as Byrd to get the plane aloft, made suggestions.

"Why don't we make the runway more slippery by sluicing water over it?" one asked.

"We could make new skis out of the whaleboat oars," asserted the other.

These projects were quickly carried out, the water that was poured on the ice instantly freezing with a sharp crackle. Arctic expert Bernt Balchen of the Amundsen expedition suggested a way to prevent another broken ski —

smearing them with a mixture of paraffin and tar.

Bennett had still another idea. He ordered the plane's tail to be tied to a stake just before takeoff. Then the engines could be revved up to top speed, insuring the fastest possible start downhill.

Tired to the bone but anxious to make this final attempt, Byrd and Bennett checked instruments, revved the three engines to their limit, signaled for the rope to be chopped by a blow from an ax, and aimed the shuddering plane downhill.

This time it shot down like a bullet, picking up speed as it glided past tense crewmen, Bennett using every trick he knew to get the plane aloft. Both men were aware that to crash at the end of the runway this time would mean the end of the plane and the expedition and could cost them their lives.

At the last possible second, Bennett pulled the yoke back and the plane's nose lifted — it was airborne! Missing the ice wall at the end of the runway by inches, it rose higher into the red-streaked Arctic sky. The thunder of the engines drowned out the exultant cheers of those on the ground.

After a two-hour test flight, Bennett brought the plane down to a smooth landing. The tired but happy pair were mauled by their companions as they squeezed out of the cabin. The next trip would be to — or toward — the North Pole.

On May 9, 1926, the weather was pronounced favorable for the epic flight. With purposeful grimness, Byrd and Bennett supervised the loading of the plane, then crawled inside. Bennett sat at the controls; Byrd was surrounded by his delicate navigation instruments.

The engines shattered the Arctic cold, the rope was cut, and the plane slid down the hill, was skillfully bounced by

Bennett at the end of the runway, and took to the air. They climbed to 2,000 feet, soaring over the glaciers and cliffs of Spitsbergen, then journeyed seaward, marveling at the vast white desolation below, broken only by streaks of dark green ocean.

For the most part, Bennett flew and Byrd navigated, taking the plane across a sky crowded with a dozen intermingling colors — a vast ceiling sometimes made more brilliant by mysterious explosions of light. Because the magnetic pole was actually south of the aircraft, making the ordinary compass useless, Byrd had to rely on frequent readings of the sun compass to direct their flight to the true pole. Every three minutes he would check wind drift and ground speed. When the plane veered off course, Byrd would signal to Bennett, who would make the correction.

All this activity required frequent changes of gloves by Byrd. As a result of this and having to take sights through his instruments through the trapdoor of the plane, he froze one of his hands and part of his face. Fortunately, the damage was not permanent. He also risked snow blindness, but snapped amber goggles over his aching, watering eyes in time.

The Arctic, the fliers saw, was not a continent but a vast sea of ice — a sluggishly moving field of white crisscrossed by an intricate pattern of pressure ridges. Able to see fifty miles in every direction, Byrd felt the exhilaration of all explorers when they come upon new, uncharted territories. All his efforts and disappointments were now repaid.

But when they were only an hour's flight from the Pole, Byrd was shocked to see oil leaking out of the starboard engine — a mishap that spelled disaster. He indicated the leak to Bennett. After glancing at the spreading oil and checking his quavering pressure gauge, Bennett scribbled hastily on a pad, "That engine is sure to stop."

Byrd stared at him questioningly. Bennett signaled that they should descend to make a landing on the ice and try to repair the engine. If the pressure fell beyond a certain point, the engine would freeze and they would have to make a landing with only two engines. Byrd shook his head. He did not want to risk a landing on the rough ice and he was stubborn enough to want to go on as long as possible.

"If we have to crash," he wrote, "it might as well be at the North Pole."

Bennett acknowledged with a grin and turned his attention back to piloting the plane. Byrd fixed his aching eyes on his charts and instruments, to determine their precise location above the desolate expanse of ice. Both expected the starboard engine momentarily to cough to a stop.

Minutes later, at exactly 9:02 A.M. (Greenwich Civil Time) on May 9, 1926, Byrd's calculations showed that the *Josephine Ford* had reached the top of the world! They were the first men to fly over the North Pole. Byrd wrote in his log, "We made it! Our dream has come true . . ." In their excitement, neither adventurer gave a thought to the danger of crashing in the white wilderness.

Byrd dashed off a whimsical suggestion to Bennett: "Let's take a trip around the world."

The grinning Bennett nodded, banking the plane in a smooth turn. The "trip around the world" took four minutes.

Byrd dropped a weighted American flag through the trapdoor, in salute to Admiral Peary. Then, as the full import of their achievement hit them, they felt, as Byrd wrote, "disembodied, no larger than a pinpoint, as remote and detached as a star."

At 9:15, after taking moving and still pictures of the

area, they headed back toward Spitsbergen, too fatigued and sleepy to fret about the leaking engine. They changed places at the controls several times, one piloting while the other dozed off for a quick nap. Once, when Byrd awoke, he could hardly believe what he saw. The oil patches on the engine were frozen and no oil was leaking out. A quick glance at the oil-indicator gauge showed him that the needle was steady. Later they learned that a rivet had jarred out of its hole; when the oil fell below that level, it ceased running out.

Finally, after hours of flying, Byrd noticed a gray smudge on the distant horizon. He shook the dozing Bennett awake. "Land ahead!" he shouted. Blinking, Bennett took the controls.

The glassy heights of Spitsbergen loomed larger and larger, and the chunky plane was soon over Kings Bay. The *Chantier*'s whistle bleated a cheery welcome. After a bumpy but safe landing on the runway, their wildly happy colleagues hoisted the fliers on their shoulders and carried them to camp. The first men to fly over the North Pole were Americans!

Roald Amundsen took time off from supervising the launching of the *Norge* to offer his warmest congratulations. (On May 11th, Amundsen himself was to fly over the Pole.) Numb from cold and fatigue, Byrd could do little but nod his thanks and grin weakly. After his frostbite had been tended to and his precious records deposited safely, he stumbled to his berth aboard the *Chantier* and flung himself down on it for a much needed nap. He was unaware of the furor his flight had caused.

Back in America, the dramatic exploit, hailed by press and radio, was the favorite topic of conversation. *The New York Times* gave him an eight-column headline:

BYRD FLIES TO NORTH POLE AND BACK
ROUND TRIP FROM KINGS BAY IN 15 HRS. 51 MIN.
CIRCLES TOP OF WORLD SEVERAL TIMES

The *Chantier,* pulling into New York Harbor, was accorded a gala welcome — crowds waving and shouting on piers, tugboats tooting their whistles, fireboats gushing water through their hoses. Byrd and Bennett were then made the center of the biggest, noisiest parade in Broadway history. President Coolidge, with the enthusiastic approval of Congress, presented the fliers with America's highest award — the Congressional Medal of Honor.

They also received the top award of the National Geographic Society, which verified Byrd's computations and confirmed his report that he had been over the Pole at the precise time he said he had been. Unquestionably, Byrd was the greatest aerial navigator the world had ever seen.

Suddenly transformed into an authentic national hero, Byrd now had to go to work. To pay back the huge sums of money he owed, he embarked on a lengthy tour of the country, giving lectures and showing films of the North Pole. Just before the tour was completed, he received a summons to the White House. There President Coolidge told him of his promotion to full Commander. Floyd Bennett, who had also been invited, was promoted to Aviation Machinist. The American Geographical Society awarded Byrd an unusual title: Doctor of Longitude and Latitude. In a citation read before Congress, the President ranked their flight with the accomplishments of Marco Polo and Columbus.

Years before, when things had looked darkest for Byrd and when his spirits had been at their lowest ebb, his father had given him a piece of advice. "A winner," he said, "is a loser who kept on trying." Thinking back over his years of struggle, his frustrations and disappointments — and now

highly respected and honored by the nation he served —
Byrd suddenly realized that his father's remark was the
wisest piece of philosophy he had ever heard.

While his flight over the North Pole was Byrd's most dramatic feat and did as much as Lindbergh's transatlantic
flight to prove the value and safety of the airplane, it was
far from his last dangerous adventure. Like the famous
Norwegian explorer Fridtjof Nansen, Byrd believed that
"Man wants to know — and when he does not want to
know, he has ceased to be a man."

On June 9, 1927 — one month after Lindbergh's famous
solo trip to Paris, and shortly after a bad crash that broke
Byrd's arm — Byrd and three companions were off on a
hop from Long Island to Paris. The purpose of the flight,
Byrd patiently explained to those who wondered why he
was following Lindbergh's route, was to show that Atlantic
crossings, while spectacular, could also be commercially
practical. Byrd's plane was the *America,* a three-engine
Fokker that carried the first transatlantic mail. Besides Byrd
as navigator, the crew consisted of George Noville, Bernt
Balchen and Bert Acosta. Floyd Bennett was unable to go
because of injuries suffered in the crackup in which Byrd's
arm had been broken.

Byrd's unpleasant experiences with overloaded planes
that risked disaster when they could not rise from the ground
inspired him to equip the *America* with the first dump valve
used by planes. In an emergency, the fuel could be quickly
dumped, lightening the plane.

"The worst thing that can happen to us," Byrd remarked
to reporters just before taking off, "is running into fog and
rain when we reach Paris." And that is precisely what
happened.

En route to Paris, he spotted a lighthouse whose needle-like beam penetrated the fog. Because a landing in complete darkness would be extremely dangerous, not only for the fliers but for the residents of the city, Byrd ordered the pilot to turn back, hoping to set the craft down near the French seacoast.

The heavily loaded plane banked in a circle and headed back through the teeming rain to the coast. The lighthouse was spotted, but vision near the ground was poor. The plane crashed into the sea, near the shore. None of the occupants was seriously injured, however, and the mail was rescued. The city of Paris, having barely recovered from the welcome it had accorded Lindbergh, took a deep breath and gave Byrd and his companions an equally fervent Gallic greeting.

While the quartet was riding in an open car beneath the famous Arc de Triomphe, Balchen took time out from smiling and waving at the Parisians lining the route to shout to Byrd over cheering, horns and music, "What's your next adventure, Commander?"

Byrd did not hesitate. "The South Pole," he answered, grinning. He imitated the movement of a plane with his hand. "I intend to fly over it."

His choice was inevitable. The South Pole was almost the last frontier on the globe. The Antarctic was reported to have the most hostile climate man had ever encountered, with winds averaging 50 knots and temperatures reaching 100 degrees below zero.

The claim made by mapmakers in the Middle Ages that the southernmost point of the world was inhabited by millions of happy, wealthy people who enjoyed a mild climate was disproved by sailors who ventured near there. Captain James Cook found his ship in constant danger from gales,

icebergs and ice packs when he sailed south of the Antarctic Circle in 1773. In 1820, Nathaniel Palmer, captain of
an American sealing vessel, reported that he saw what
could be the icy rim of a continent — a cold, barren expanse that the American Government was not enthusiastic
about claiming. In 1909, the American explorer Ernest
Shackleton struggled against numbing cold and blizzard to
come within 90 miles of the Pole, but the hardships were
too great and he was forced to turn back. Amundsen succeeded in reaching the South Pole two years later.

To take care of the endless details involved in mounting
an expedition, Byrd set up headquarters in New York City
as 1927 came to a close. His main problem, once again, was
money. An encouraging amount was sent in by school-
children, including a contribution of $4.35 from his son
Dickie. Again, most of his support came from Edsel Ford
and John D. Rockefeller, Jr.

Byrd cut expenses to the bone, buying two old trawlers
which he had overhauled and refitted for the trip. He decided
he would need three ski-equipped monoplanes. One of them
was an all-metal, three-engine Ford plane — donated by
Edsel — that could fly 122 miles an hour and carry a load
of 15,000 pounds. This equipment, plus over 600 tons of
various kinds of cargo and the purchase of 100 Eskimo dogs,
burdened the explorer with a debt of $100,000 when he
finally left America for his assault on the South Pole.

It was a shattering blow to Byrd that his friend Floyd
Bennett could not accompany him on the trip. But Bennett,
in flying to rescue two German aviators who had made a
forced landing in Newfoundland, had caught pneumonia.
Despite the cooperation of Lindbergh, who flew serum to
Bennett from New York, Bennett died suddenly and unex-

pectedly. His last request was that Byrd should drop his flying scarf over the South Pole.

On August 25, 1928, the larger of Byrd's two supply ships, the *City of New York,* departed for New Zealand. The *Eleanor Bolling,* named after Byrd's mother, followed a month later. After making their rendezvous, the ships sailed east and south, running into gales and rough seas which were the fiercest any of the crews had ever seen. Riding low in the water because of the weight of the cargo, the ships were nearly torn to pieces by the shrieking, violent winds. The *Eleanor Bolling* was sent back to New Zealand for repairs, but the *City of New York* kept on.

When the ice pack surrounding the Antarctic continent was reached, a large, sturdy whaling boat was hired to knife a path through the pressing ice so that Byrd's ship would not be halted or crushed. Finally the awesome 100-foot-high ice cliff that forms the rim of the continent — the Ross Ice Barrier — was sighted. The ship sailed east until it came to the Bay of Whales, a breach in the barrier thirty miles wide.

Little America, Byrd's camp, was set up there during a severe snowstorm, with curious penguins watching the men and dogs as they labored.

A month of exhausting work passed before Byrd took to the air for the first time. Then, experiencing his old feeling of exhilaration, he made his first exploration by air, flying over a mountain range which he named the Rockefeller Mountains. A few more flights to test machines and the accuracy of his instruments, and the eerie black Antarctic winter set in. At his suggestion, they dug in in caves chopped in the ice, as safe as possible from 150-knot winds that cut across the continent with hardly a moment's warning.

At the end of the Antarctic winter, like bears after hibernation, the bearded crew dug itself out and made Byrd's plane ready for the flight over the Pole.

At 3:29 P.M. on November 28, 1929, the Floyd Bennett, with Bernt Balchen at the controls, made a smooth takeoff and headed at a speed of ninety miles an hour toward the South Pole. Hal June was copilot and radio operator, Ashley McKinley was the aerial photographer, and Byrd was the navigator.

Through the minds of all ran one question: Did the plane have enough power to climb the 11,000 feet necessary to clear the Axel Heiberg glacier? This glacier was one of the gateways to the polar plateau which stood between them and the Pole.

After nearly six hours of flying, the Heiberg Glacier loomed ahead — and the altimeter read only 9,000 feet. To the right was the Liv Glacier, another pass to the plateau. Byrd made a quick decision. Although the height of the Liv Glacier was unknown, the plane had to head for it; any other course would be disastrous for the straining craft.

The four suddenly felt a bumping and lurching as vertical air currents buffeted the plane. Balchen nudged the throttle forward, trying to gain altitude, fighting for control of the ship. He realized that the plane would not be able to pass over the glacier. A crash seemed inevitable.

"We've got to lighten the plane!" he shouted. "Throw two hundred pounds overboard!"

June looked questioningly at Byrd.

"Throw out a bag of food!" Byrd ordered.

As frigid air shrieked into the plane and the sack shot down toward earth, the plane shot upward.

Balchen made a quick estimate. "Get rid of two hundred pounds more!" he shouted.

Byrd nodded, and the last of the food was tossed out. With only inches to spare, the plane swept over the glistening peaks of the glacier. For 300 miles more, the plane droned on above the plateau as Byrd shot the position of the sun, determined drift and ground speed, and repeatedly corrected the plane's course.

By his calculations, it was 1:14 P.M. on November 29th that the plane circled over the same historic point on the globe that Amundsen had reached and so many explorers had died trying to reach. Filled with emotion, Byrd opened the trapdoor and dropped a stone from Floyd Bennett's grave. Around the stone was Bennett's scarf, and attached to it was an American flag.

"There it is, Floyd," he murmured as the objects fell away to land in the desolate white landscape below. "The way you wanted it." Then he gave the order to turn back toward Little America.

Richard E. Byrd made other Antarctic explorations by air. He gave the name Marie Byrd Land (after his wife) to one immense, hitherto unexplored, area. He named a mountain range after Edsel Ford. Blasting through the ice, scientists in his party found coal in the Queen Maud Range. This was proof that the Antarctic had not always been cold and in earlier times had been warm enough for vegetation.

Once again, on his return to America, Byrd found himself a national hero. Congress elevated him to the rank of Rear Admiral. A special Congressional medal was designed and awarded to all members of his expedition. President Hoover, in a speech welcoming him back to the United States, said in part, "You have given us proof that the spirit of adventure still lives."

In the years that followed before the outbreak of World War II, Byrd made three more trips to the Antarctic. He built Little America II on top of Little America I, and in 1939 set up Little America III.

"If I live to be a hundred," Byrd stated, "I won't have

enough time to thoroughly explore those five million square miles."

In awarding him the Legion of Merit, President Franklin D. Roosevelt praised Byrd for his contributions to the fields of navigation, aviation, exploration and other important sciences.

Although Byrd was fifty-two years old when America entered World War II, he performed valuable service for the armed forces as a locator of bomber and naval bases in the South Pacific, and was an authority on cold-weather clothing and equipment. In the European Theatre, he became an expert on planning coordinated air-ground attacks. He was aboard the U.S.S. *Missouri* when the Japanese surrendered in 1945. His final war service was inspecting and reporting on atom bomb damage done to Hiroshima and Nagasaki.

Given the title of Admiral of the Antarctic, Byrd in 1948 flew past the South Pole to penetrate the vast reaches that lay beyond it — a flat, barren surface speckled with ridges of hardened snow.

In March, 1955, President Eisenhower announced that Byrd would be in command of Operation Deepfreeze — the most intensive study of the Antarctic yet undertaken. When Phase I had been completed, Byrd returned to the United States, too weak, at the age of sixty-seven, to withstand the rigors of the Antarctic.

One of his major ambitions had been to establish a permanent American base at the South Pole — the first ever set up there. He was too ill to supervise the work in person, but he had an important hand in its planning. White-haired and thin, at his home in Boston, he received the welcome news that a scientific observation post had been established at the South Pole.

Fittingly, on March 11, 1957, when news of his death

reached the men at the bottom of the earth, the American flag was lowered to half-mast as a hostile wind howled in the dusk and a great explorer was saluted by his comrades.

A month before, when Byrd had been awarded the Medal of Freedom by the Secretary of Defense, the citation read, in part:

By virtue of his unparalleled experience, he has made a unique contribution to the Antarctic expedition over the past three years, the development of permanent Antarctic legislation and international scientific understanding and good will. He has exercised his special talents in the promotion of the United States interests in the Antarctic with foreign countries and has personally laid the ground work for the present large-scale Antarctic effort of the United States. These accomplishments represent a lifetime of service which has encompassed unequaled exploits of skill, daring and imagination, including a flight across the Atlantic Ocean, the initial flights across the North and South Poles, and five historic expeditions to Antarctica. His actions and performances of these duties have been in keeping with the highest traditions of the United States Government Service.

CHARLES A. LINDBERGH
Aviator

He was terribly afraid of heights. In his youth and even as a young man, he had vivid dreams of plummeting down from high places, helpless, paralyzed with fear. There were other fears he had at night — nameless fears until, in desperation, his mind gave them shape: a snake waiting to strike; a slavering beast in the jungle; a murderer with a strangling cord.

In the reassuring light of day, as though to prove that fear was foolish and could be conquered, he took risks that were foolhardy in the extreme. One afternoon in Little Falls, Minnesota, when he was fourteen, he clambered atop a sixty-foot elm tree and calmly announced to a friend below that he was going to jump.

"Don't do it!" his friend anxiously shouted back. "You'll kill yourself!"

Charles — he was not yet called Slim — gingerly made his way out to the end of a limb that curved dangerously under his weight. He had the reputation of carrying out his pronouncements.

His friend, greatly alarmed, shouted warnings so loud that Charles's mother came running out of the house. Frightened for his safety — he was her only child — she ordered Charles to climb down. Her voice carried authority.

Charles hesitated, set his lips in a straight line, apparently debated his decision — and then slowly began to climb down. He always did what his parents told him, and there might be chances for future jumps. When he had climbed to within ten feet of the ground — perhaps to salvage some of his pride — he flung himself from the tree. He let out a loud grunt as he landed flat on his back. He was shaken up but not hurt.

Charles's father, C. A. Lindbergh, was deeply involved in politics and believed more in the power of words than in physical punishment. Neither parent had ever struck Charles, but that night he came very close to getting a thrashing.

The following day his friend asked him if he really would have jumped.

"I think so," said Charles in his quiet, thoughtful way. "I almost felt I had to."

As he grew older the compulsion to risk his life and limb in the face of common sense persisted. Indeed, it was a kind of medicine; he found he always slept better after daring something rash. When he attended the University of Wisconsin in Madison, his main interests — aside from competing on the rifle team — was riding a motorcycle at breakneck speeds. The narrower and twistier the path, the more slippery the surface, the faster he went.

One day he and two other students were strolling down

CHARLES A. LINDBERGH

a street that bisected a very steep hill. Running parallel to
the bottom was another street, its far side bordered by a
strong wire fence.

Casually, one of his companions guessed that a motor-
cyclist could never make the turn at the bottom of the hill
if his brakes didn't work. "He'd smash right into the fence,"
he concluded.

Charles disagreed. He had considered the problem and
felt that the sharp turn could be made without brakes.

His companion shrugged. "We'll never know," he said.

Charles was determined to prove himself right. The following day as his alarmed friends stationed themselves at
the bottom of the hill, he pushed his cycle to the top and
wheeled it around. Panting a little, he straddled it and
started the engine. His friends watched apprehensively as
he pushed off, quickly gathered speed, and roared down the
hill. He did not touch his brakes.

Gathering momentum, the cycle bounced and chattered
toward the fence at the bottom. Charles's speed was too
great. Unable to make the turn, he crashed hard into the
fence. He escaped injury except for cuts and bruises.

It was inevitable that he immediately try the stunt again.
Back he went up the hill with his cycle. This time, having
learned what he had done wrong on his first run, he gunned
his vehicle as he made the 90-degree turn, missed the fence
by inches, and roared on down the road, triumphant in the
knowledge that his estimate of what the machine could do
had been correct.

In his junior year, he planned to hoist his cycle to the
top of the campus ski lift, soar down the snowy slope at its
steepest part, and tool away, if no accident occurred, onto
the smooth ice of Lake Mendota. Fortunately for American

93

aviation, he left school before he got around to trying that experiment.

It is safe to say that during his life as a venturesome youngster, as a wing-walker, a barnstorming pilot and an experienced aviator, Lindbergh escaped death several hundred times. He came closest to being killed as a parachutist — the parachute of the early 1920's being far removed from the soundly engineered device it is today.

Shortly after leaving college, he got a job selling rides for a group of barnstorming airmen — "gypsy fliers," they were called. A person who took a flight in their scary contraption had something to talk about for months. While watching a rival air show, he had become fascinated with the stunts of Charles W. Hardin. A friendly little man with a mustache, Hardin was a balloonist and a parachute pioneer. He convinced prospective customers that the chutes he made were safe by wearing them for his jumps. One of his stunts involved the use of two parachutes: he would hang from the wing of a plane at 2,000 feet, drop off and allow one chute to open; then he would cut it loose with a knife, free fall for a few hundred feet, and open a second chute.

Lindbergh's terror of heights compelled him to ask Hardin to let him jump. Characteristically, Charles did not want to do a conventional jump but the advanced double drop — multiplying the risk by at least two.

Hardin was astounded by the request. "On your first jump?" he demanded.

Lindbergh scuffed the ground with one shoe and stammered that he might want to become a professional parachutist himself. Hardin remembered his own youthful urges to tumble out of a plane and soar, however briefly, in the air. There was, too, a kind of philosophy that airmen and would-be airmen shared: returning from the border of death makes one more aware of life. Hardin agreed and prepared the chutes for the double jump.

A half-hour later the twenty-year-old Lindbergh was in the front cockpit of Hardin's biplane as it circled above the ground. As might be expected, he was rapidly losing his courage; the jump would be, he realized, a nightmare made real. The pilot, having gone as high as he was going, tapped Lindbergh on the shoulder and indicated that he should jump.

As chill air pierced his lungs and lashed his cheeks, Lindbergh climbed out onto the wing and fumbled with the chute straps, affixing them to his harness. Then he hung from the wing, the ground below a quilt of fields and woods. He was fearful of falling, yet having gone this far, felt he must fall.

A last deep breath and he let go, plunging earthward. The first parachute flowered up over him, and he felt the sharp jerk of the risers when it took its gulp of air. He knew relief and exaltation as his speed was checked and he swayed back and forth below the large white canopy. It was time to cut away the first chute, and regretfully, he did.

This time, however, there was no comforting upward jerk of the risers. He tumbled head over heels for several seconds — seconds that seemed like hours to the perplexed young man. Why didn't the second chute open? It finally struck him that it would never open, and he quietly resigned himself to dying. The dreams, then, must have been a warning.

Suddenly he was startled to see the canopy over his head slowly fill with air. His descent was checked. Once more exaltation replaced dread and he floated to earth.

After he landed, a white-faced, shaken Hardin told him that he had been sure the second chute would not open — none had ever taken that long to open before. It developed that the second chute had been improperly tied; because of this, it had remained folded. Presumably, it was the merest chance that it had opened at all.

Never one to brood over dangers past, Lindbergh shrugged off his near miss with death. What had remained with him, he said later, had been confidence gained by his ability to let go of the airplane wing. The double drop had proved his second greatest challenge.

Growing up in Little Falls, Minnesota, Charles Lindbergh was a typical loner. He was a shy, gawky youngster, avoiding social gatherings. He did not like the standard recreations of skating, fishing or hunting. Despite the fact that his blue eyes, tousled blond hair, straight nose and finely molded chin made him attractive to girls, he simply was not interested in their company. Indeed, he seemed much less engrossed in people than in machinery; machinery, for him, had a personality and vitality that human beings did not.

He drove a noisy motorcycle up and down the town streets and took apart and put together again the family cars — first a Ford and then a Saxon. At school, he did well in mechanical drawing, poorly in nonscientific subjects. He was always fond of practical jokes — a characteristic he retained well into adulthood. Undoubtedly his most famous grammar school prank was catching a dozen flies and attaching them, one by one, to a straw. Then he carefully placed his masterpiece in the aisle and sent the entire squad marching down toward the teacher. It took the bewildered lady half an hour to restore order in the class, and Charles had to stay after school for several days as a penance.

After graduation from high school, being descended from a line of farmers, Lindbergh tried his hand at farming. He found it arduous and unprofitable work, and decided to study mechanical engineering at the University of Wisconsin. In the three years he spent there, his marks were only fair and he resented frequent examinations and being forced to attend classes. Clearly, time spent in schools was wasted. But he might have earned his degree if he had not found something more fascinating to absorb his attention.

Up to his junior year in college, he had seen only two airplanes. He had been thrilled, of course, by the exploits of World War I aces in their Jennys and de Havillands, and even more so by the daring flight from Newfoundland to Ireland, in 1919, of Captain John Alcock and Lieutenant Arthur W. Brown.

But so enthralled was Charles by speed — he had lately taken up iceboating — and so bored was he with the academic life, that he decided to become an aviator. Quite naturally, his father disapproved, and so did his mother (flying was popularly considered a profession for madmen), yet neither wished to deny their son the right to choose his own field. And so, after looking over several advertisements for flying schools, he decided on the Nebraska Aircraft Corporation in Lincoln, Nebraska — an airplane factory at which aviation was taught as a sideline.

Curiously enough, as far as learning to fly was concerned, Charles could hardly have made a poorer choice. At the factory, he watched planes being assembled, even helping out with boyish enthusiasm. He also made his first flight in a factory product — certainly the biggest thrill of his life up to that time. But when it came to actually learning how to pilot a plane, it looked as though the $500 he had paid for the "course" had been thrown away.

There was only one instructor and only one student — the slender, six-foot-three young man whom people were now calling Slim, despite an appetite of prodigious proportions. The instructor, having seen a friend killed in an airplane crash, wanted to have nothing to do with planes, flying or students.

Lindbergh often arrived ready for a lesson only to find the instructor absent. On some days the instructor postponed his appearance until the weather was too blowy for flying. In a two-month period, Lindbergh received only eight hours of flying instruction, most of it reluctantly given. Yet he retained his eagerness, felt a peculiar exaltation when at the controls of a plane piercing the sky, and longed for the time when he could buy his own machine.

Halfway through the course, he was suddenly informed that it was over. The plane used for training was to be sold to a businesslike but skillful aviator named Erold Bahl, who was about to conduct a barnstorming tour through Nebraska.

Angrily, Lindbergh demanded to be allowed to solo and thus obtain his flying certificate. Despite the few lessons he had received, he was confident he could handle the trainer. The corporation, unwilling to risk the loss of the plane, flatly turned him down. Lindbergh, white with anger, stormed out of the office and located Bahl.

He explained that his money was gone and he was still not a flier. Bahl was a sympathetic listener but he could see the corporation's point of view: planes were too valuable to be entrusted to callow youths.

"How about my joining your barnstorming tour?" Lindbergh blurted out on a sudden impulse.

Bahl hesitated. Profits were small, no one would sell insurance to an aviator, and the young man glowed with inexperience.

"Sorry, kid —" he said.

"I'll pay my own way!" Lindbergh said, in desperation.

Bahl allowed himself to be convinced. There would be no drain on his budget, at least, and the young man just might be useful.

The second phase of Lindbergh's flying instruction began. His main job was urging members of the crowds attracted by Bahl's acrobatics to take rides in the plane after Bahl bounced in for a landing. A flight was such an adventure at the time that the passenger immediately became a kind of local hero.

Then Bahl was surprised at Lindbergh's request to be allowed to climb out on a wing of the plane as it buzzed over the crowds. Despite his fears, Lindbergh felt the stunt would not only attract greater crowds but would help convince them that flying was not the crazy enterprise they imagined. Bahl offered Lindbergh some tips about wing-walking and gave his consent.

The stunts were so successful that Lindbergh tried others — hanging from a rope tied to the landing gear, and when another plane and pilot were available, jumping from one plane to another in midflight. He had very little trouble sleeping. Crowds were wildly enthusiastic, and Bahl put him on salary.

When the tour was over, daily risks had become a kind of drug to Charles. He immediately joined another barnstorming troop, adding to his repertory of suicidal tricks. He repeatedly made double and delayed jumps by parachutes and stood on top of a wing while the plane looped the loop. He became known as Daredevil Lindbergh. By the time late fall came, he had saved enough money to convince a banker that he could be trusted for the rest. In Miami, for $500, he bought a 90-horsepower two-seater Curtiss Jenny, able, in good weather, to go 70 miles an hour.

At the airport, the happy salesman counted the money

and waved Lindbergh to the plane. "Think you can take her up?" he asked, not knowing that his customer had never soloed — or indeed had never flown a Jenny before. Getting her down might present a more difficult problem.

Lindbergh climbed into the rear cockpit, certain that he could, with a little practice, become used to the Jenny. At least no one could now prevent him from *trying* to solo. A mechanic whipped the propeller around, and the engine caught.

Lindbergh started skimming over the ground, the Jenny much more responsive to the controls than the training ship in Nebraska had been. The tail rose, the wheels were off. Suddenly losing his confidence, he thrust the stick forward to bring the plane down. Its wheels slammed on the runway so hard that it bounced high in the air, nearly jarring him out of the cockpit. The machine he had been so anxious to purchase was about to be wrecked by his impetuosity. The next bounce was slighter and so was the third. Finally the plane was rolling along the runway.

I need lots of practice, he told himself as he nervously taxied back to the hangar, aware that disapproving looks were being thrown his way. Probably "crazy kid" was the kindest of the names he was being called.

A pilot who had finished his day's flying offered to instruct him in the strange workings of the Jenny, and Lindbergh gratefully accepted. So well did he adapt himself to the controls that when evening fell his instructor did not argue when Lindbergh announced that he was going to solo. And he did, as the Florida sky grew gray with approaching night. He was too impatient to wait till morning — though he had never landed a plane without an instructor in the cockpit.

In the dimming sky, he flew high over fields and towns

and lakes — higher than he had ever flown before. He felt greater freedom than he had ever known. There was adventure and exhilaration in each cloud he passed through, in the cold streams of air that caressed his cheeks. This, he realized, was what he was meant for.

It was nearly dark when he brought his plane in. He had put himself in the position of making the most difficult type of landing possible, but that was the way he did things. The greater the risk, the greater the satisfaction.

Now he became a barnstormer himself — at a time when flying was the most dangerous profession in America. There were extremely few airfields. When gas was low or engines stalled, pilots were forced to bring their planes down in cow pastures, grain fields and even village streets. Almost the first qualification for a pilot was having a keen eye for relatively safe emergency landing places; no radio helped him find his bearings if he got lost. After the plane put down, cows or mules might eat the fabric covering the rubber, which they found delicious. Cactus sometimes punctured the tires on landing. Teams of horses often had to be used to pull planes out of deep mud. Rough landings broke propellers, wheels and wings, and these had to be sent for and shipped to where the plane lay — a process that often took weeks. When the parts arrived, the pilot had to do his own repair work. Often the ground was too soft for taking off, in which case, to achieve sufficient speed, the plane had to be pushed by dozens of volunteers from nearby villages and farms.

In the Twenties, the American aviator had to be mechanic, hiker, goodwill merchant, daredevil and first-aid expert. It is small wonder that the pilots of that decade felt a kinship among themselves and found it difficult, as bird-men, to communicate with people who did not enjoy the perils, problems and discomforts of flying.

Lindbergh's program was simple. He would fly over a town, doing wingovers, loop-the-loops and barrel rolls in his underpowered plane, to make his presence known. Then he would set his plane down in a field, and after crowds assembled, make his pitch: a ride in the air for a dollar a minute. During this phase of his life he had three minor crack-ups, slept in haystacks or under a wing of the plane at night, and landed in swamps. Once, trying to pass between two telephone poles only inches farther apart than the Jenny's wingspread, his wing tip caught. The plane did a slow turn, crashing into a hardware store. The owner was delighted, asserting that the "free advertising" would triple his business.

Lindbergh barnstormed north as the weather got warmer. In Minnesota, while waiting to take a passenger up, he was given some advice that changed the course of his life and gave him, for the first time, a definite goal. It came from a young graduate of the Army Air Service Training Schools. Looking at Lindbergh's patched-up Jenny in some perplexity, the youth advised Lindbergh to try to enlist as an Air Service cadet.

"These Jennys are dangerous," he told Lindbergh, who, despite his affection for the plane, was not unaware that it handled clumsily, even in good weather. "As a cadet, you'll fly high-powered planes."

"De Havillands?" Lindbergh asked.

"And Hispano-Suizas." The youth nodded.

It was enough for Daredevil Lindbergh. As he looped the loop with a daring passenger, he resolved to become an air cadet.

At Brooks Field and Kelly Field in Texas, he went

through rigorous training for twelve months — the best and most disciplined education a flier could get anywhere in the world. The Army figured that flying was risky enough without entrusting its planes to any but the most competent and resourceful of pilots. Of his class of 104 cadets, Lindbergh was one of 18 who did not wash out. He finished second from the top, and except for playing practical jokes and stunting with valuable Army property more than he should have, readily subjected himself to the discipline of the school.

In the powerful de Havillands, he passed tests such as landing, after a deliberate stall, inside a prescribed circle on the ground, and doing figure eights over landmarks a hundred feet apart. He learned dogfighting, combat strafing and light bombing. His favorite maneuver was diving vertically for thousands of feet in close formation with other pilots; it helped appease his appetite for danger.

The most dramatic thing that happened to Charles at the school was being crashed into by another plane during a simulated dogfight. Calmly, he watched the other pilot jump as the entangled planes whistled toward earth, and then, after checking his parachute, jumped himself. It was the first time anyone had escaped alive from an airplane collision in the air. Within an hour, he and the pilot whose plane had hit his were flying again.

He was now a pilot in the Army Air Corps Reserve, subject to call in a national emergency but otherwise his own man. After barnstorming for a few months, he was asked to become chief pilot for a St. Louis company that had been awarded an airmail contract by the government. By present-day standards, the route was a short one — between St. Louis and Chicago — but weather factors, particularly at night, made the trip dangerous.

Lindbergh was the ideal pilot, the company reasoned, for the desperate kind of flying necessary to get the mail through. In those days of mistrust of airplanes and when a company's reliability was on trial, getting the mail through — despite sleet, fog, thunderstorm and blizzard — was the company's major concern. Lindbergh hired two other pilots, selected sites for landing fields between the two cities, and made the inaugural flight to Chicago.

It was during one of these flights, in the fall of 1926, that he first began to consider flying the Atlantic. The subject was one that had been given serious thought in certain circles for many years. In 1919, a dramatic announcement had been made: Raymond Orteig, a French-born American hotel owner, World War I veteran, and admirer of aviators, offered a prize of $25,000 for the first pilot to fly non-stop from New York to Paris or from Paris to New York. The offer was to stand for five years. During this time, so formidable did the 3,600-mile flight seem that, though considered, it was never attempted. In 1926, Orteig extended the limit another five years. With more powerful engines and sturdier, better-designed planes available, dozens of pilots contemplated the project, undiscouraged by one of the great air tragedies of 1926.

The greatest of French war aces, René Fonck — with a crew of three in a large biplane especially designed for the flight — roared down the runway of Roosevelt Field on Long Island. But the plane was so overloaded with gasoline and accessory equipment that it could not rise from the ground. Neither could it stop. It crashed into a gully at the far end of the runway and burst into flames. Fonck and his navigator escaped but two crewmen were burned to death.

As Lindbergh considered making an assault on the Atlantic, he was quite aware that he faced imposing competition in the race to be first: Commander Richard E. Byrd, the polar explorer, planned to make the flight in a Fokker with a three-man crew; Captain Fonck was going to make another try; attempts were about to be made by a pair of Naval airmen in a Keystone Pathfinder; and by Clarence Chamberlain in a Bellanca. In France, England and Italy, pilots were also preparing planes for the long journey.

During the next few days, while fighting storms over Illinois, Lindbergh thought over the problem, learning a great deal from his study of the Fonck disaster. Fonck's plane had had three motors — but a single-engined plane would need less gas and would also weigh less. The plane itself should be stripped to the barest essentials to decrease overloading to a minimum. If a single man made the flight instead of three or four, extra pounds of fuel could be carried.

But the flight would take at least forty hours. Could a pilot stay awake that long — completely awake? Charles reflected. Of all the problems, this seemed the greatest. An instant's carelessness at the controls, and he might crash his plane in the vast, chill Atlantic. But during his barnstorming days he had stayed awake (though not always in the cockpit) for that length of time. Everything considered — it might be possible. Because of the weight factor, one man might succeed where several would fail. Perhaps the solitary nature of the long flight appealed to him, too.

The idea took possession of him, and for weeks he thought of little else. He needed money, of course, and this problem would be much greater for him than it had been for men of renown like Fonck, Byrd and Chamberlain. Nor was his late start in what had developed into a highly competitive race especially helpful.

Fortunately, his needs were modest, and when he presented his plan before St. Louis businessmen, they loaned him $13,000, to which he added $2,000 of his own. If he won the Orteig prize, the money would be repaid; if he failed to win it, the money would never be returned.

Lindbergh searched in vain for weeks for a firm that would build him a plane for $15,000. Finally, after much frustrating negotiation with well-known aircraft firms, he visited a tiny company in San Diego. So discouraged was he by continuous rebuffs (some of his rivals were ready to take off, and he did not yet have a plane), that he even thought of trying to fly the Pacific instead of the Atlantic. There was little competition for that, at least.

At the dilapidated plant in San Diego — Ryan Airlines — he was promised a plane for $6,000 plus the cost of the engine. The price was reasonable, but he had doubts about the company's ability to turn out a plane to his rigid specifications. The only thing in this company's favor was that it seemed as down-at-heels and hungry as he was; the members would work as hard as he would to get the difficult job done.

His associates in St. Louis gave their approval and the deal was closed. As the plane began building, when he was not studying navigation, Lindbergh carefully supervised its construction. Despite the objections of the company designer, he insisted that the main fuel tank be placed on top of the fuselage in front of the pilot's seat.

"But how will you see anything?" the designer demanded.

"I'll look out over the side," Lindbergh answered. In a crash, he did not want to be trapped — as many pilots had been — between the engine and the fuel tank.

Shrugging, the designer drew up blueprints to Lindbergh's specifications.

CHARLES A. LINDBERGH

After two months of backbreaking work, the plane was ready, powered by a 220-horsepower, 9-cylinder, air-cooled Wright Whirlwind engine. Silver-gray, carrying oversized wings, it was christened, in honor of the businessmen who had backed him, the *Spirit of St. Louis.*

Test flights followed as he accustomed himself to the controls with the plane bearing ever-increasing loads. Finally he was ready to fly it east — and he impulsively decided to try to break some speed and distance records while doing it.

The plane responded perfectly to his demands. He broke the speed record from San Diego to St. Louis and, arriving on Long Island, the transcontinental speed record as well. For the first time, the American public began to take seriously the quietly determined Charles A. Lindbergh.

Paradoxically, while Lindbergh's chances of successfully making the transatlantic flight grew, those of his main rivals sank. Chamberlain's attempt was delayed by bitter internal struggles within the Bellanca Company; Byrd's Fokker crashed on its first test, seriously injuring Floyd Bennett, his pilot; the pilot and copilot of the *Pathfinder* were killed when their plane failed to rise over trees at the far end of the runway; and two famous French pilots, after leaving Le Bourget Field in Paris, mysteriously disappeared at sea.

On Thursday, May 19, 1927, the weather over the northeastern part of the United States was especially unfavorable for flying. Rain came down in sheets, reducing visibility to zero, making runways soggy. In a hangar at Curtiss Field, Long Island, teams of experts checked over the *Spirit of St. Louis,* and the pilot himself carefully examined every nut, bolt, cam and spark plug in the engine.

There seemed to be no chance of flying, so he and some friends started to drive to Manhattan to see a show. After a

107

few minutes on the road, Lindbergh told the driver to stop.

"I think it's clearing," he said after squinting at the sky for a long moment.

A friend volunteered to get out and phone the Weather Bureau. When he came back his face was wreathed in a grin.

"You were right, Slim," he said, climbing in. "It's clearing up all along the coast and over Newfoundland. And it even looks good far out over the Atlantic. I guess we'd better turn around."

"I guess we had," said Lindbergh, with the shade of a smile.

As fast as the driver dared, they sped back to the hangar, where preparations were made for fuel to be poured in the tanks and for the plane to be towed to nearby Roosevelt Field. Roosevelt had a longer runway than Curtiss, and fresh in Lindbergh's mind were memories of crashes caused by overloaded planes trying to take off from runways that were too short.

Weary from tension and concentration on a thousand details, he went to a nearby hotel to sleep late that night. But sleep, that precious commodity, would not come. Charles tossed on his bed, thinking about the problems of the flight as rain pattered against the window. He was to be awakened a few hours later, at 2:15 A.M., but lying in bed was so depressing that he decided to get up ahead of time. He took a bath, shaved and dressed. In the lobby, reporters badgered him with questions but he shook them off and hurried to the car that was to take him to the airport. He noticed that while the rain was coming down less hard, the stars were still obscured by clouds.

Braving the rain, a large crowd waited for him at Curtiss Field, watching silently as he gave the order to haul the plane to Roosevelt Field. He followed in a closed car. At Roosevelt, he got word that the weather was clearing over New England and Newfoundland. Byrd and Chamberlain came over to wish him luck, noticing — as did Lindbergh — how the plane's tires bulged under its heavy load. It was carrying over 5,000 pounds — more than it had ever lifted before.

The hazards of taking off loomed large: the runway was soggy, the plane was clearly overloaded, and a shift in the wind meant that getting off the ground would be even more difficult than he had figured. He could hardly ask for a greater challenge.

Lindbergh put on his flying suit over his clothes, and donned helmet and goggles. In the cockpit he found two canteens of water and five sandwiches. To save weight, he had dispensed with a parachute and a toothbrush.

It was nearly eight o'clock. Beams of light began to filter through the rising clouds; mist over the runway began to dissipate. At his signal, a mechanic heaved the propeller around and Lindbergh opened the throttle wide. The plane roared and shook; needles on the instrument panel quivered. The tachometer told him that the propeller was not making as many revolutions per minute as it should. An additional handicap! For a brief moment, doubts ate at his confidence: would he, like the others, fail because he could not get the plane off the runway?

The chief mechanic was standing by.

"How does she sound to you?" Lindbergh shouted above the engine's roar.

The mechanic hesitated, looking uncertain. Then, in a hearty voice said, "She sounds okay to me."

Lindbergh stared at him. Everything rested on his, the

pilot's shoulders. Challenges, he told himself, existed to be defied. He must stay calm.

"Then I might as well go," he said.

It was 7:52. The blocks were removed from the wheels, and the plane, exploding with sound, was pushed along the soggy runway. Taking a fresh grip on the stick, Lindbergh opened the throttle to its widest, and the plane picked up speed, leaving behind the men who had been pushing it. Sluggishly, it lumbered down the miry runway. Finally the tail was up. Faster and faster it sped. There was no turning back now; Lindbergh was committed to taking off. His face pale and drawn, he eased the stick back. The wheels were off the ground. Now he was climbing higher — over telephone wires, a line of trees, Below him, in the weak shards of daylight, he could make out a sea of upturned faces as white as his own. The *Spirit of St. Louis* became a tiny thing in the vast immensity of sky. Charles was headed for Paris.

The world's attention was fixed on the lonely flight. In an age of assorted heroes, Lindbergh — if successful in a venture most people thought suicidal — had the qualities of a genuine one. He was modest, good-looking, brave. He neither smoked nor drank. He seemed possessed of a quiet confidence which was the envy of all who met or read about him.

People along the route of his flight toward the coast filled the streets to get a glimpse of his plane. They listened to radio reports of his progress. They shuddered when, mistakenly, it was flashed that he seemed to be having engine trouble.

Charles passed over Connecticut, Rhode Island and Massachusetts. After flying over Nova Scotia, he rose high into the air to avoid storms, and zoomed low again while over Cape Breton Island. Citizens of St. John's, the capital of Newfoundland, caught sight of him as he passed overhead, heading for a gap in the mountains to the east.

Now he was over the Atlantic. Newfoundland's mountains disappeared; ahead of him were spots of fog. On the dark waters below he could make out streams of icebergs. The fog increased in thickness; clouds pressed in on the plane.

He climbed desperately but could not escape the enveloping clouds. He dove into inky blackness 10,000 feet above the ocean. Completely blind, he shone his flashlight through the cockpit windows and was unpleasantly surprised to find ice forming on the wings. Ice was a more dangerous enemy than clouds; its weight could plunge him into the black ocean below.

In a maneuver that would have astounded most pilots, he made a long, slow turn, checking his altimeter, and headed back toward Newfoundland. Somewhere near there, he reasoned, he might find an area of sky where no cloud blanket blocked his vision and no icy pellets fell.

The change of course worked. Suddenly finding himself under bright stars, Lindbergh made another long, slow turn, resuming his way to Ireland. On he tracked through the immensity of sky, over thunderheads, past fluffy pillars of clouds, awed by the grandeur that surrounded him.

He felt warm and comfortable — and sleepy! Startled out of his drowsy complacency, he slapped his cheeks and concentrated on solving his navigational problem. Anything to keep from dozing. He tried smelling salts and found they had no effect. He ached with fatigue. There was nothing to do but fight it.

The moon rose and soon, it seemed to him, dawn came.

Sometimes he flew ten feet above the ocean; sometimes he soared high above it. The sun beat down on his open cockpit, and the noise of the engine helped keep him awake. Toward nightfall he suddenly noticed boats — fishing boats.

He soared to within fifty feet of a crew member and shouted a question: "Which way is Ireland?"

Receiving no answer except a dull stare, he climbed again, certain that land must be near. Shortly afterward — after flying for twenty-eight hours — he saw land: green hills, rocky islands. He recognized Dingle Bay, in the southern part of Ireland. He was precisely on course, despite his detour, his not always accurate compasses. Six hundred miles away was Paris.

Charles sped across the green hills of Kerry, the hedge-lined fields of Cornwall, the English Channel. Now he was over France — Cherbourg, the peninsula on the western coast.

He followed the coastline south, then banked left as he reached the Seine River. Below him, French citizens ran into the streets and stared upward; he was reminded of American crowds staring up at him on Long Island. Suddenly remembering that he had not eaten since leaving America, he tasted one of his sandwiches. He did not enjoy it; fatigue combined with tension had robbed him of his appetite.

Night fell as he sped over the Seine to Paris. He recognized the Eiffel Tower, and flew around it before heading toward Le Bourget Airport.

Where Le Bourget should be, he made out a black square bordered by lights. Was that it? He came down to 1,000 feet, circled and lost more altitude. The dimly lit field seemed too small to hold his plane. He plunged down against the wind, numb with weariness, into the dark area, completely unaware of what might lie in front of him.

Lower and lower he came, trying desperately to see by sticking his head outside the cockpit windows. Finally the wheels touched down, then the tail. He tooled along the runway, immensely satisfied with his machine. It had done the impossible. In Paris, it was Saturday, May 21st and 10:22 P.M. Lindbergh cut the engine.

Suddenly he was amazed to see a gigantic crowd press toward him, shouting out his name: *Lindbergh! Lindbergh!* Now, curiously, he was to begin to pay the penalty for his heroism. Screaming worshipers surrounded him, lifted him bodily in the air, and refused to let his feet touch the ground. Souvenir-hunters tore the fabric of the plane and pried away pieces of wood. Helpless, he watched in dismay.

A pair of French aviators pushed through the tide of packed humanity and saved him, one of them tossing Lindbergh's helmet into the crowd, as a distraction. As the crowd battled for it the pilots seized him, set him on the ground, and hustled him to a car. He was taken to a dark room in a hangar, safe from the attentions of his admirers. After being reassured that his plane would not be destroyed (it, too, was rescued), Lindbergh was taken to the office of the airfield commandant, and there introduced to the American Ambassador to France, Myron T. Herrick.

"Young man," said the Ambassador to the aviator who presented to France an image of America that Frenchmen had never seen before, "I am going to take you home with me."

"Thank you," replied Lindbergh with a faint smile. "I'm rather tired."

In the days that followed, he reacted to the public glare with a poise and dignity that few had suspected he possessed. Presumably, it was still another challenge. He made

113

speeches, received medals and gave interviews. After cementing the friendship of France and America, he flew to England and charmed the English, who were as wildly ecstatic as the French.

Charles sailed back to America on the flagship of the U.S. Fleet and was greeted by the biggest ticker-tape parade in history. "The Big Blizzard of 1927," it was called.

For his feat, he received much more than the Orteig prize of $25,000. President Coolidge commissioned him a colonel. He was sent around 500,000 letters and 75,000 congratulatory telegrams. Songs were written about his flight. The movies wanted him; record companies wanted him; he received offers of $5,000,000 to endorse products. (He turned them all down.) Crackpots wanted him to fly to Mars, and inventors wanted him to invest in their ideas, such as making gold from seawater.

Many poems were written about his bravery. His psychological effect on people was analyzed by a Washington newspaper: "Women," it said, "sought to take this man and embrace him. The men . . . thought wistfully of things they might have done, things they would like to do, things they wished they had the nerve to do." Operas were written about his flight. He could hardly step out on the street without being pursued by a screaming mob. And all during this ordeal of deification, no hero could have reacted more sensibly, patiently or heroically.

In the years that followed, he made goodwill tours to Latin America and the Orient, married Anne Morrow, the daughter of an American ambassador, preached the future of aviation, and urged America to keep pace in the air with the countries of Europe.

Turning to other fields, he dabbled in archaeology and helped develop an artificial heart. During World War II, while in his forties, he flew pursuit ships, shot down two Japanese planes, and showed American pilots how they could economize on fuel — an important tactical factor in the war in the Pacific.

But Lindbergh's place in history revolves around his "suicidal" flight from Long Island to Paris. Single-handed, he demonstrated to the people of the world how the world had shrunk, and dramatized the reliability and the wonders of the flying machine. The boy who had been afraid of heights became the greatest hero of the 1920's, and it is safe to say that he advanced the cause of aviation more than any man before or since.

J. EDGAR HOOVER
Lawman

It was May 10, 1924. Two men sat on opposite sides of a large desk in the office of the Attorney General. The person behind the desk, a tall and heavy-set man, was Harlan Fiske Stone. Just two months previously, President Calvin Coolidge had appointed him Attorney General; now he was to make an appointment of his own.

Stone's job was not an easy one. A New York attorney, a former dean of Columbia Law School, he had brought a reputation for firmness and integrity to the office he now held. The country still rocked in the wake of the scandals that had broken Warren G. Harding's Administration. Misled by friends, taken advantage of by political cronies, the late President Harding had been unable to cope with the

117

corruption that was so widespread during his time in office.

This corruption had run wild through the Department of Justice. Harry Daugherty, former Attorney General, had been forced to resign in disgrace, and had left behind him a department overrun with political appointees and inept bunglers. Now Harlan Fiske Stone had the task of cleaning house. He had to weed out crooks and incompetents, and at the same time gather around him the men who could best serve as the core of an honest and efficient Justice Department.

The man sitting across the desk from Attorney General Stone was an important figure in his plans. Only twenty-nine years of age, he had been with the Justice Department for seven years and had remained uncontaminated by the widespread corruption.

His name was J. Edgar Hoover.

Stone looked long and hard at him. "Mr. Hoover," he said finally, "I've got a big job for you. I want you as Acting Director of the Bureau of Investigation."

For a moment Hoover said nothing. He had half expected to be fired when he first entered Stone's office: heads were falling left and right, and Hoover could not be sure that Stone would not want to replace him with someone new — someone who had not been previously connected with the scandal-ridden department. Now, instead of dismissal, he was being offered a top spot.

Hoover outlined his words carefully before replying to Stone. Then he accepted the job, but not without conditions. The bureau he was to head would have to be politically independent, he told the Attorney General; it could not be a catchall for political appointees. Both appointments and promotions must be based on merit, and Hoover and his men would be responsible to Stone and to no one else.

"I wouldn't want it any other way," Harlan Fiske Stone told him. "The job is yours."

The job was his, but it was to be hard work with little glory. Neither the job nor the Bureau itself were anything like what they are today. The Bureau of Investigation itself was not even a shadow of the highly efficient, professional, universally respected organization it has become over the years. Its duties and powers were only vaguely understood at best; its agents were improperly chosen and poorly trained.

Actually, the Bureau was even younger than the man who had been placed at its helm. As recently as 1908, the Department of Justice had lacked a branch to handle Federal investigations. From time to time, an Attorney General might borrow Secret Service agents from the Treasury Department. In 1908, however, Congress passed a bill which made this kind of borrowing impossible: an Attorney General could no longer place any men at his command when an investigation seemed necessary.

President Theodore Roosevelt realized that the situation was an impossible one. He issued an executive order for the formation of a service within the Justice Department itself to handle investigative work. A year later, when Roosevelt was succeeded by William Howard Taft, the bureau he had created was maintained and given a title — the Bureau of Investigation. (Its present name, the Federal Bureau of Investigation, did not come into existence until 1935.)

The new bureau went to work without anyone knowing too clearly what it was or what its duties were to be. When World War I broke out, the Bureau suddenly found itself with a job on its hands: it was faced with the responsibility of combating espionage on a great scale and of keeping tabs on the enemy aliens living in the United States.

There were over 100,000 enemy aliens living in this country at the time, and there were about 300 men working for the Bureau. Their resources limited, the Federal agents faced an impossible task. On top of this, they had to contend with a great wave of sabotage, both on the part of German agents and by native American radicals who opposed American participation in the war.

The Bureau could not cope with the task that confronted it. In the few years since its organization, it had been weakened by the addition of agents who were appointed as political favors. There were dedicated men in the Bureau — men with a keen interest in honest law enforcement — but they were lost in the shuffle.

As act upon act of sabotage drew public attention, some men proposed a unique scheme to aid the Bureau in its duty. A group of misguided patriots volunteered as vigilantes, organizing citizen committees to rout out saboteurs and spies. These vigilante bands soon ignored civil liberties entirely. Some of them did little more than hire themselves out as strikebreakers to help unscrupulous employers put an end to labor union activity.

Vigilante activity was not encouraged for long, but while it went on, it did nothing to aid the good name of the Bureau. And later, in the years just after the war, the Bureau again ran into heavy fire during the so-called Palmer Raids: widespread public fear of radicals and Communists flared up in a series of raids in which Federal agents seized left-wing aliens for deportation.

The Red scare that followed the war marked the first real public recognition of the menace of Communism at home. But the wholesale roundup of alien radicals was marked by a total disregard for civil rights and due process of law as men got carried away by what they saw as their duty. Men were deported, not for having done anything, but for their political views.

It was in the course of the Palmer Raids that J. Edgar Hoover first began to come into prominence. He had been born on New Year's Day in 1895, and educated in public schools. He graduated from law school at George Washington University in 1916, by which time he had already entered government service — beginning as a page at the Library of Congress in 1913. He spent another year earning his Master's degree in law, then joined the Justice Department in July of 1917.

During the war years Hoover had been placed in charge of a unit in the enemy alien registration section. Now, in 1919, he was made head of the General Intelligence Division of the Bureau as a Special Assistant Attorney General charged with the task of making a study of subversive activity in the United States.

As Hoover studied the theories and activities of various radical movements working within the nation, he became more and more firmly convinced that Communism represented a serious threat to the future of the country. While other parties and movements were native American political organizations, Hoover clearly saw that the American Communist parties were directly linked with the new Communist Government in Soviet Russia. Communism, he realized, was not merely a political movement; it was a conspiracy. From this point on, Hoover's determination never flagged: he did not lose sight of the threat of Communism over the years, and always remained its firm and dedicated opponent.

He also proved his own personal value to the Bureau. People were beginning to take notice of J. Edgar Hoover, to appreciate the true merits of this young lawyer. His courage and honesty were unquestioned, and his ability proved itself again and again.

When the Harding Administration came into power, Harding's crony, Harry Daugherty, was rewarded with the post of Attorney General. It was then that the position of the Bureau took a dramatic turn for the worse. Hoover found himself transferred from his Special Assistant post and made an Assistant Director. William J. Burns was brought in to head the Bureau, despite the strong opposition of organized labor and the fact that Burns had been involved in earlier scandals. Political hacks and party followers replaced hard-working Bureau operatives. Along with the rest of the Justice Department, it sank deeper and deeper into corruption and public disrespect.

Hoover went on working, fighting the enemy of lawlessness as well as he could under these conditions. Alarmed by the growing vigilante power of the Ku Klux Klan in the South, he launched an investigation in which Federal agents infiltrated the Klan and helped expose its excesses and illegal acts. The Klan's political power in the South was tremendous during the early years of the Twenties, and few politicians had been willing to risk its opposition. But Hoover was not a politician. He was a lawman, and political considerations did not deter him. While the Klan remained strong for several years, the publicity which Hoover cast upon it did much to line up public opinion against the Klan and pave the way for its decline.

During the Harding years, young J. Edgar Hoover looked at the Bureau around him and dreamed of what it might become. Lawlessness was spreading throughout the country, and state and local officials were often powerless to deal with criminals. Gangsters, organizing to supply illegal whiskey during Prohibition, were getting an increasingly greater grip on local power. Bank robbers and hold-up men, equipped now with high-speed armored cars, were able to hit and run, escaping across state lines and leaving a trail of death and destruction behind them.

The country needed Federal law enforcement and needed it badly. And yet a Federal police force must be run properly. Under the wrong conditions, such a force could quickly degenerate into a secret police organization such as the dread Russian GPU. Hoover had a vision of what the Bureau ought to be — a balanced picture of the ideal Federal law-enforcement organization. Yet when he looked around him, he could only see a corrupt and inefficient bureau dominated by politicians and filled with incompetents.

And then Harlan Fiske Stone replaced Daugherty, and on that day in May of 1924, Hoover had the chance for which he had been waiting. The Bureau of Investigation had been placed under his command. It was his to reorganize, his to remodel along new lines. It would be a new bureau, free of political encroachment, free to grow modern and efficient and responsible. He had the opportunity, and he was resolved to make the most of it.

Some men are a natural target for biographers. Their lives are filled with dramatic incidents; their personalities sparkle with color and excitement; and the stories of their lives make fascinating reading.

But other men, every bit as important and exciting, do not lend themselves to biography. When you take a long look at these men, their lives seem to be completely a part of their work, and their personalities seem completely absorbed in their organizations.

This has been the case with J. Edgar Hoover. From the moment Attorney General Stone entrusted him with the leadership of the Bureau, Hoover's life has been completely bound up with it. In a sense, the history of the FBI has been his biography. Anyone who wants to know his life story must look for it in the annals of the Federal Bureau of Investigation.

For the first three years after his appointment, Hoover devoted himself to the reorganization of the Bureau He and Stone worked out a body of rules. The Bureau was to operate entirely as a fact-gathering organization, with its investigations strictly limited to Federal matters. Investigations would be made under the direction of the Attorney General; incompetent agents would be systematically weeded out and dismissed; the size of the Bureau would be kept as small as possible. Finally, no new men would be appointed without the approval of the Attorney General. While political hacks might have found their way into the Bureau in the past, they would not remain there now — and no new political appointees would replace them.

Step by step, Hoover put his program into effect. In the past, each Bureau agent had taken his orders and made his reports to Washington. Now Hoover established chains of command, with agents reporting to their local special agents The agents themselves must be neatly dressed, well-man nered, and of good personal character. Hoover was often criticized for his actions in this area — some people complained that he was running a Boy Scout troop instead of a Federal bureau. But he knew that the Bureau must be above criticism if it was to be effective. Every agent was responsible for preserving the good name of the organization as a whole.

While he molded the men around him into an upright and efficient force, Hoover worked also to increase the Bureau's capacity for effective action. Its laboratory became the best in the world for scientific crime analysis. The fingerprint section, constantly expanded over the years, was geared to make possible the identification of anyone who had ever been fingerprinted anywhere in the country. And its training academy was established and improved to the point where Bureau training was unparalleled anywhere in the world. The men whom it turned out were as well equipped as they could possibly be for the problems they would face.

Throughout the Twenties and in the course of the years to follow, Hoover's men struck blow after blow at the forces of crime. Some of their work was directed inward at the machinery of the Federal Government itself, in an effort to expose and correct corrupt conditions.

In his first year as the head of the Bureau, Hoover discovered that conditions in the Federal Prison at Atlanta were unbelievably bad. The warden was using his power to fill his own pockets, and a rich prisoner at Atlanta could get anything he wanted if he was willing to pay for it: he could buy his way out of his cell and roam around the city itself; he could buy a soft job inside or outside the prison; and he could equip his cell with all the luxuries of life outside. While the warden and his men grew rich, the prison administration sank deeper and deeper into the mud.

Hoover's men investigated, delving into prison operation, talking with one prisoner after another until a full picture of conditions at Atlanta began to emerge. The Bureau's report turned Atlanta Prison upside down: the warden and his leading henchman went to jail for taking bribes; the prison chaplain was removed from his post; and the entire system of managing and operating the penitentiary was completely overhauled.

In 1926, the Bureau moved in another direction when stock swindlers organized the Bankers Trust Company, also in Atlanta, and set up a bubble that caused losses of

$10,000,000 and closed 86 banks throughout the South when it burst. Bureau of Investigation agents worked hand in hand with Post Office inspectors, developing a solid case of mail fraud against the swindlers. In the past, it had been all too easy to get rich selling worthless stock; there were few government regulations in existence, and those that did exist were difficult to enforce. Later, during the early years of the New Deal, a whole body of regulations would be drawn up to protect the public against swindles of this nature. In the meantime, Hoover was determined to do what he could.

When the case was over, four of the leading officials of the Bankers Trust Company were in jail, but the top man had escaped the trap. He was in a private rest home in Georgia, certified by his physician as mentally incompetent and unable to stand trial.

Bureau agents would not let the case drop. One of them quietly went under cover and had himself committed to the rest home where W. D. Manley was staying. He became friendly with him and took extensive notes of Manley's conversations. Before long, a sanity hearing for Manley was held, and the Bureau's agent's notes were introduced as testimony. Manley was ruled sane, went to trial, and was sentenced to seven years in prison for his role in the stock swindle.

In case after case, Hoover's men went on proving themselves as able fighters against crime. The going was not often easy. Time after time, Bureau agents would run into trouble when the roots of a criminal conspiracy extended into local politics. Often the local police refused to cooperate, and often local politicians would do everything they could to discourage or head off an investigation. But the

Bureau's operatives stuck to their guns, and Hoover backed them all the way.

He quickly saw that the rise of organized crime was going to be a problem the Bureau would have to meet face to face. The criminal gangs of the Prohibition era — gangs which had sprung up to furnish liquor to millions of thirsty Americans — were steadily spreading and building an empire of crime. They took over gambling and the drug trade, and as their profits grew, they gradually muscled in on legitimate business as well.

The gangsters could not be dealt with on a local level. They bought politicians and rigged elections; they bribed police officers by the hundred. On many levels they were an increasingly terrifying menace to the country.

Naturally, the Bureau could only move against them when a Federal law had been violated. In many cases it was powerless to act, but whenever the gangsters operated in violation of Federal law, Hoover's men could enter the picture. They moved against Al Capone, kingpin of Chicago crime, time and time again. Bureau investigation slapped the gangster into jail on a contempt of court charge. This kept Capone behind bars for six months, enough time to permit Internal Revenue men to take a close look at Capone's financial records. By the time he was out of jail, the revenue agents were ready. The gangster was charged with tax evasion, sentenced to ten years at Alcatraz, and stayed there until his death.

In Cincinnati, Bureau agents moved in when corruption spread through the ranks of Federal Prohibition agents and engulfed the entire city. Federal laws were being broken right and left, and the Bureau had the right to investigate. By the time it was through, Cincinnati had been turned inside out. Seventy men — police officers and prohibition agents — went on trial for their activities; sixty-two were convicted. A wave of reform swept the civic administration out of office and paved the way for a top-to-bottom shake-up in local politics.

Hoover's force began to win respect throughout the country. Gangsters took pains to avoid breaking Federal laws — they knew that Bureau men could not be bought and could not be scared off. But there were men who were not so pleased with the Bureau or with the man at its helm. And many felt that the Bureau would not maintain its quality. After all, they reasoned, J. Edgar Hoover had been appointed to his post by a Republican attorney general. When the Democrats took over in 1933, would Hoover be out and the Bureau drift back to its former self?

If this had happened, it would have meant the defeat of everything Hoover had worked for. Perhaps another man might have been able to fill his shoes, but that was beside the point. The main issue was that Hoover had worked to keep the Bureau free from political control. If each succeeding President felt free to change the leadership of the Bureau of Investigation, it would once again be an instrument of politics.

When Franklin Delano Roosevelt took office in 1933, Hoover's enemies happily awaited his dismissal. They got a surprise. Roosevelt recognized the importance of the Bureau and appreciated the value of Hoover's leadership. J. Edgar Hoover remained in office.

And in 1934, Roosevelt pushed through new legislation that would make the Bureau equal to the task of fighting the great wave of crime that was sweeping the country. A quick succession of bills was hurried through Congress and signed by the President. These laws made it a Federal crime to assault or kill a Federal officer or to rob a Federal bank. Fleeing across a state line after commission of a crime, or carrying stolen property across a state line, was also a Federal offense and would enable the Bureau to enter a case. These bills and others greatly increased the jurisdiction of the Bureau of Investigation, enabling Federal officers to concern themselves with countless crimes that had formerly been out of bounds for them.

And the agents' powers were increased as well. They were allowed to carry guns — formerly they had needed special permission. They were given full power to make arrests. At last Hoover had the opportunity to fight criminal activity on an equal basis. It was an opportunty he had wanted and he did not fail to take full advantage of it.

The years were lawless years. It was during the late Twenties and the early Thirties that the face of crime in America changed greatly. Just as gangsters had brought a new look to organized crime and corruption, so did bandits and bank robbers revise crime throughout the Midwest. Outlaws like John Dillinger, Pretty Boy Floyd and Baby Face Nelson, mobs of hoods like Ma Barker's gang and Machine-Gun Kelly's mob, terrorized parts of the country.

They were outlaws of the Old West equipped with modern weapons and transport. Instead of six-shooters, they blazed away with machine guns and high-powered rifles. Instead of riding horses, they cut across state lines in armored cars with powerful engines. They killed wantonly, looted systematically, and utterly defied the efforts of state and local law-enforcement officials to curtail their activities.

To J. Edgar Hoover, these criminals were an outrage. The money they stole, the lives they took, were not the only considerations. As long as criminals could run uncontrolled, no one in the nation could feel truly safe.

Armed with their new powers, Bureau agents went to work. Machine-Gun Kelly, the notorious ex-bootlegger whose favorite weapon gave him his nickname, kidnaped a man in Oklahoma City in July of 1933. Brilliant detective work by Bureau operatives uncovered the identity of the kidnaper and set the Bureau on his trail. Kelly was tracked to Denver and trapped in his hideout.

He threw his gun aside. "Don't shoot!" he called out. "Don't shoot, G-Men!"

A dangerous criminal had been captured — and the Bureau agents had a new nickname of their own.

One by one, they worked their way through the ranks of desperate men. John Dillinger, bank robber and leader of an especially vicious gang, escaped from jail with a toy gun and fought his way clear of dozens of attempts at capture. Hoover's men caught him in Chicago, once again combining careful, plodding investigation with equally careful attack. A tip led the Bureau to set a trap for Dillinger in a Chicago theatre. Agents staked out the area, and when Dillinger left the theatre, he was surrounded. He went for his gun — and three Bureau agents shot him down in an alley.

The record of the Bureau's cases during this period of time reads like a history of crime. Over a period of several years, its agents hunted down one criminal after another, sending man after man to jail or to death. It broke the Barker-Karpis mob man by man, with Hoover himself on the scene for the capture of Alvin Karpis in New Orleans. It cornered Baby Face Nelson in a pitched battle that ended with Nelson dead. It ran down Pretty Boy Floyd — another man who had been responsible for the deaths of Bureau agents in the past — and killed him in a gun duel.

That was part of the battle. The reign of terror had to be broken, and the criminals who were preying on the country had to be rounded up and jailed or shot down and buried. But Hoover knew there was another side to the story. The sudden wave of lawlessness could not have come about without a public willing to look the other way. And criminals could not escape capture so long without police officers who would take bribes and fail to make arrests.

Hoover spoke out. He saw that far too many average Americans were glorifying the bandits and killers instead of seeing them as the hoodlums that they were. Dillinger had become a national hero in the eyes of many. Someone had written a sentimental ballad extolling the virtues of Pretty Boy Floyd, a song that attempted to make a Robin Hood out of a murderous bandit. And Baby Face Nelson's widow had given out interviews that made her husband seem like a saint who had been foully murdered by beastly Bureau men.

Hoover took time out to make speeches and give interviews. He lashed out at criminals, calling them the scum of humanity, pounding away at the principle that anyone who glorified lawlessness or protected a criminal was sharing the crook's guilt. He hammered away at the civic corruption that made some cities "safe towns" where criminals could hide out with no fear of arrest. He attacked parole boards that were too quick to return hardened criminals to society.

Hoover's words found listeners. The men in his command did their own jobs and did them well. Before long, the tide had begun to turn. The great resources of the Bureau of Investigation — its scientific laboratory, its fingerprint file, its dedicated agents and its tenacious leader — had made the "new look" in crime far less attractive. Professional criminals began to realize that bank robbery was passé, that any crime that would draw the attention of the Bureau was exceptionally dangerous.

The Twenties are long gone. Prohibition is barely a memory. The scandals of the Harding Administration are almost ancient history. That day in May of 1924 was a long time ago, but the man who was placed in command of the Bureau that day still fills the same spot. Presidents have come and gone. Crime and subversion have worn many faces. But J. Edgar Hoover remains at his post.

Every year, the Federal Bureau of Investigation grows stronger and more completely a part of the American system of law enforcement. Every year the Bureau sticks to its policy — investigating, keeping a lid on crime and conspiracy, yet never permitting itself to grow too strong and never becoming in itself a threat to American freedom.

No agency of the government has ever been so completely a product of one man's work. J. Edgar Hoover has been a part of the Bureau, just as it in turn has been the deep and abiding passion of his life. Since his appointment under Coolidge's Administration, every American President has seen the wisdom of keeping this man in office.

He was, far and away, the leading lawman of the Twenties. And he has gone on to be the leading lawman of the century.

JACK DEMPSEY
Fighter

On a blistering hot July 4th afternoon in Toledo, Ohio —
ringside temperature was 110 degrees — not many fight
fans thought the beetle-browed, scowling ex-hobo had much
chance against the gigantic Jess Willard, world's heavyweight champion.

The year was 1919, when ladies' skirts were long and
hugged their ankles, and ladies' hats were monstrous and
top-heavy. The country gloried in having settled the Kaiser's
hash in "the war to end all wars," and boxing — in some
states at least — was taking on a mantle of respectability.

One sign of it in Toledo was the presence of a few brave
women among the shirt-sleeved, straw-hatted, perspiring
males in the vast crowd. Not yet emancipated, the ladies
were much quieter than the tensely waiting males. Together,

they made up the biggest gate in prizefighting history, with ringside tickets selling for an unheard-of $60.

The unquiet men, fanning themselves with their stiff hats, mopping faces with damp handkerchiefs, readjusting gay sleeve garters that threatened to cut off circulation, shouted dire predictions of what the Pottawattamie Giant would do to his comparatively small challenger. Now and then a bet would be made, but Willard backers had to give odds like 8–5 and 2–1. Never did the maxim, "Always bet on the champ," make better sense.

The challenger was 62 pounds lighter than the 250-pound ex-cowboy; he gave away 5 inches in height and at least that in reach. Then there was the matter of reputation — Willard's was impressive. Discovered and nurtured as a "White Hope" — a large, tough white man who might take the title away from Jack Johnson, the Negro who held it — Willard had knocked out or won decisions over a dozen other white hopes. To the surprise of almost everyone, in a bout held in Havana, Cuba, Willard had knocked out Jack Johnson — the champion who was considered the greatest fighter of his time, the large black man who had cut ex-champion Jim Jeffries to pieces in Reno a few years before.

The new heavyweight champion had then successfully defended his crown by jabbing another giant, Frank Moran (famous for his hard right uppercut), to the point where Moran was swinging like a dervish in the late rounds. Willard won an easy decision. Earlier, Willard had killed a man in the ring — Bill Young — a fact which enhanced his reputation but curbed his appetite for knockouts.

Willard's jab, combined with his reach, was his most formidable weapon. "He'll jab the punk silly," was the consensus of the wise money. Certainly the challenger, if he chose to move in on the stately Willard to trade punches, would take a terrible beating around the head. And Willard was hard to knock off his feet. The few times he had been stung by body punches — as by Soldier Kearns — a rage had enveloped him and he had punched his foe all around the ring, heedless of the punishment he was dealing out. He had also taken, for 26 rounds, the best shots Johnson could throw at his jaw; apparently Willard had one of the toughest chins in the business.

As for the ex-pool hustler, ex-saloon fighter, who was he? He had won some fights by quick knockouts, but most of his victims were unknown to the average fight fan. He was widely regarded as a tough young pug — an unknown quantity heralding from the Far West. If his punches, particularly his left, landed, he could hurt you, but he had to land first.

Only a few months before, he had lost a 4-rounder to Willie Meeham, a fat, funny little man who seemed always to be able to outbox and outthink sluggers. On the positive side, Dempsey was known as an aggressive fighter who did not mind taking three punches if he could land one good hook. He paid little attention to picking off blows, relying on a cast-iron jaw to withstand punishment, and a bobbing-weaving style of moving about the ring that made it hard for opponents to set him up for a solid punch. His style also confused some of his opponents, who were never sure from what direction his damaging hooks would come.

Dempsey was a hungry fighter — one of the hungriest who ever lived — and those who had seen him fight in the past two years recognized him as a tremendous crowd-pleaser. Those who had seen him, in fact, were apt to forget all about Willard's size and reach to put their money on Dempsey.

It was so hot in the arena that the resin boiled out of the

bleacher seats. Warm water, described by hawkers as iced, sold while it lasted for a dollar a glass. Lemonade, however, was not finding many takers. The sun poured down so hotly that Battling Nelson — the former lightweight champion — had jumped into the hogshead containing the liquid, and using plenty of soap, had taken a bath in it.

In Dempsey's sweltering dressing room, the nervous challenger paced up and down, an old robe slung over his shoulders. He slapped one taped fist into the palm of his other hand, developing a rage against Willard. It was a common prefight ritual for Dempsey. All the frustration, pain, degradation and misery he had experienced in the past rose inside him, filling him with bitterness. A little later the rage would find release in his fists.

Dempsey's manager, Jack Kearns — the most ring-wise and cunning of all prizefight managers — tried to act casual, though he felt almost as tense as Dempsey. The fight for the title was something that both had been seeking for a long time. For his chance at Willard, Dempsey had accepted a small purse — $19,000, as against Willard's $100,000.

"Real anxious crowd out there," Kearns told him as stamping and clapping noises penetrated the dressing room door.

Dempsey threw him a dark look and continued his pacing, jabbing and hooking at the air.

"Take it easy, Jack," said Kearns nervously. "Save some of that for Willard."

"Maybe you're right." Dempsey stopped shadowboxing and dangled his arms at his sides. He seated himself on the table, his robe clutched around his shoulders. Perspiration coursed down his well-tanned shoulders and chest. "I never seen it this hot," he murmured in his almost unintelligible Far-West accent.

Jack smiled slightly, thinking about an extra grievance he had against Willard. A few weeks before, Jack had been driving his new Stutz Bearcat along an Ohio road and had noticed a big Cadillac in front of him. Jack honked, but the driver refused to pull over to let him pass. Angrily, Jack pushed the throttle and came up beside him, nearly careening into a ditch when the road suddenly narrowed. The driver, he noted in surprise, was the huge Jess Willard. Jack scowled, gunned his engine and roared past, risking an accident. But no one was going to bluff Jack Dempsey.

Without knocking, Tex Rickard, the promoter of the fight, pushed open the door. He was the picture of wealth, smoking a large black stogie and brandishing a gold-headed cane.

"How do you feel, Jack?" he asked.

"Hot," grunted Dempsey. He beckoned to his second to toss him a towel so he could wipe his face.

Rickard came closer, showing concern. "Listen, Jack," he said. "I'm worried about this fight."

Kearns and Dempsey stared at him.

"Jess is big and strong," Rickard continued. "I don't think you know just how strong. He killed a man, remember."

"We heard," snapped Kearns. "Get to the tag."

"I wouldn't want to risk your getting hurt bad, Jack," Rickard said in a friendly way. "What I think you ought to do is, if he belts you a hard one, go down and stay down."

This was unusual advice for a promoter to give to a challenger and Dempsey suddenly found it hard to breathe in the heat. Sensing an explosion, Kearns leapt toward Rickard and steered him toward the door, gushing out a flow of words — the meaning of which was that Dempsey had trained hard and carefully for the fight and was in the best condition of his life. Rickard did not have to worry about Jack's getting hurt, but maybe he should get out before someone else did.

"Good luck, Jack," Rickard called as the door was slammed in his face. Before Kearns could comment on Rickard's advice, a boxing official stuck his head in and told Jack it was time to enter the ring. Jack's chief sparring partner, Big Bill Tate, led the way, followed by Jack, Kearns and Jack's second, trailed by his trainer. A cheer swelled and broke — not so much for Dempsey as in anticipation of the excitement that was to come. Dempsey slipped through the ring ropes a few minutes before four o'clock.

To burn off excess energy, he tugged at the ropes and danced a few steps on his toes. "Where is he?" he demanded of Kearns after a few minutes of waiting. He was keyed up to the point where further delay was torture. He had hardly slept the night before, he was so eager to meet the champion.

Finally a gigantic roar announced the presence of Willard, followed by his entourage. Gasps and laughter mingled with cheers when it was seen that his sparring partner, Walter Monahan, was shielding the champion from the sun with a pink parasol.

Willard's hair was neatly plastered down — in sharp contrast to Dempsey's, which was cropped so close that his skull showed. There were other differences. Willard's body was white and loomed huge compared to Dempsey's when the two stood in opposite corners of the ring. Willard was clean-shaven; Dempsey, to give his face a grimmer, more tigerish look, wore a pronounced stubble. Willard sat at ease in his corner, a placid giant. Dempsey's eyes wandered over the crowd on all sides, then came to rest on Jess, and the scowl he wore deepened.

The referee, Ollie Pecord, called the fighters to the center of the ring and sputtered out instructions. It was his first championship fight and he was understandably nervous. Jack was amazed at how hard and muscular Willard looked in spite of his great size.

The bell rang, and with a roar of anticipation, the crowd rose to its feet. Dempsey charged from his corner, then stopped short. Willard's face showed surprise as Jack went into a deep crouch, his head tucked behind his left shoulder. He had not rushed out swinging, as Willard's advisors had said he would. Recovering, Willard flicked out a series of jabs and Dempsey bobbed clear. He jabbed again, disconcerted by Jack's lack of aggressiveness, and Dempsey slipped the punches.

For almost a full minute, that was the pattern of the fight: Willard the pursuing aggressor; Dempsey the elusive target. Then suddenly Dempsey exploded. He took a jab on the forehead, feinted a left to Willard's body, and when Willard thrust down an elbow to block it, hooked a vicious right to Willard's cheekbone. The punch, it developed later, was one of the hardest ever thrown in the ring. It shook Willard to his toes.

As was his fashion, Dempsey never gave his opponent a chance to recover. He threw rights and lefts in furious succession at Willard's body and head, and it seemed he couldn't miss. It was like a wildcat attacking a slow-moving majestic elephant. One punch blasted Willard's left eye open; others raised lumps on his jaw. Finally Jess tumbled down like a gigantic tree.

Unbelieving, the crowd stood on chairs and screamed itself hoarse. Willard slowly rose to his feet and was promptly smashed down again by a flurry of Dempsey hooks and uppercuts. His face bleeding from a dozen cuts, Willard took the count on one knee and pushed himself up a second time. Now Dempsey was in frantic pursuit as Willard stumbled about the ring, trying to protect himself with elbows and gloves. But Jack was a keen marksman, as well as boxing's hardest hitter. Down Willard went. He got up and was knocked down again. Never had a champion taken such a beating in the ring. Once more he went down, flopping to a sitting position in one corner. This time, glassy-eyed, dazed, he could not struggle to his feet. Pecord's count reached ten, and an ear-shattering cheer rose for the new champion.

Or was he the champion?

In the strangest set of circumstances in the history of boxing, Dempsey was nearly declared the loser. As he pushed his way down the aisle, ecstatically happy, arm weary from throwing punches, accepting congratulations and slaps on the back, Dempsey was surprised to be clutched by Kearns, who was screaming at him.

"What?" Dempsey whirled around, his face filled with consternation.

"Get back in the ring!" Kearns screamed. "The fight's not over." It was several seconds before Dempsey could be made to understand. Incredibly — though no one had heard it but the timekeeper — the bell had been sounded before Pecord's count reached ten. The round had ended before Willard had been counted out. Given the information by the near-hysterical timekeeper, Pecord had grabbed Kearns and shouted to him that the fight wasn't over. Kearns, verging on apoplexy, argued and stormed, but Pecord insisted that Dempsey would be disqualified and would forfeit the fight if he did not return for the second round. Kearns looked aghast for a moment and then tore down the aisle after Jack.

A bewildered Dempsey hauled himself inside the ropes for the second time. Willard, slumped on his stool, showed a right eye puffed and closed, two front teeth missing, his

140

face bulging with purplish lumps and a badly swollen cheekbone.

As the bell rang, summoning the fighters to the center of the ring, Dempsey felt both discouraged and weary. He came out cautiously, trying to conserve energy. Willard was no more anxious than Dempsey to trade punches, so the round ended with little damage done by either fighter.

The third round, however, was different. As the bell rang, Dempsey sprang forward off his stool, aware that he must finish Willard quickly or the giant, who showed great courage and endurance, might prove too strong for him.

Jack ran into a straight right by Willard — Jess's best punch of the fight — and his head flew back with a jerk. A terrific roar went up and part of the crowd stood on their seats. Slowed only momentarily, Dempsey leapt forward again, the killer he had been earlier. Rights to the heart, lefts to the chin, hooks to Willard's battered body — and when the bell clanged, Willard had to be led away to his corner.

Dempsey sat on his stool, near exhaustion. His hands were heavy and air passed harshly in and out of his lungs as he took deep gulps of the torrid air.

"One more round and he'll go down," Kearns predicted, kneading one of Dempsey's calves as a second held a bottle of water to Jack's lips.

"He better, or I will," Dempsey gasped.

The bell rang and Dempsey, summoning an extra reserve of strength, pushed himself to his feet. But there was no Willard for him to fight. The Pottawattamie Giant sat slumped on his stool, unable to come out for the fourth round. A second tossed in the towel, forfeiting the fight. Pecord walked over to Dempsey and raised his arm in victory. He was heavyweight champion of the world.

Completely exhausted, Dempsey flung himself into bed at about ten o'clock that night. He had a terrible nightmare — that Willard was battering him all over the ring and finally knocked him out. Jack awoke in a cold sweat, got up and anxiously turned on the lights. He stared at himself in the mirror. There was not a mark on his face. He threw on some clothes and ran down to the street in front of his hotel. A newsboy was hawking papers on the corner. Dempsey hurried over to him.

"Listen," said Dempsey. "The fight this afternoon. Who won it?"

The kid stared at him. His face lighted up. "Say, you're Dempsey, aren't you?"

Dempsey nodded.

"You won, you dope!"

Vastly relieved, Jack gave him a dollar and went back to the hotel and to bed.

Few events can change the course of a man's life as suddenly and dramatically as winning the heavyweight championship of the world, the most admired title in all of sports. No longer the grim, unknown challenger, Dempsey was now catapulted into the public eye. And he was a champion who thoroughly deserved the adulation heaped on him. He had won the title after many disappointments and eight years of getting pounded by bigger men for tiny purses.

Not a large man compared to most of his opponents, he was the fiercest hitter ever to step in the ring, the best at infighting and the most dedicated to destroying an opponent. Only Joe Louis could finish a man off more efficiently than Dempsey. And only Bob Fitzsimmons was a more effective body puncher.

The three-round "Massacre of Toledo," as the fight came

to be known, made a national hero out of a former hobo. It was to give boxing its biggest shot in the arm since an enterprising cave man found that a doubled-up fist was a fair substitute for a wooden club.

Dempsey was the first of the immortals of the Golden Age of Sport — the decade between 1920 and 1930 that was made colorful by the exploits of Babe Ruth, Ty Cobb, Red Grange, William T. Tilden, Helen Wills, Bobby Jones, Walter Hagen, Knute Rockne and his Four Horsemen, and Gertrude Ederle.

Oddly enough, Dempsey faced his biggest struggle after beating Willard. He was not only under the public microscope, but was the companion of the rich, the talented and the famous, and he had to shape his habits and image to conform with what was expected of someone of his stature.

The changes he had to make were staggering. He had to learn to speak properly and to dress the way a champion should. He had to get used to wearing neckties, which he hated. On the advice of Jack Kearns, a fancy dresser, Jack also wore a derby hat and a coat with a fur collar. He took up ballroom dancing but never became good at it. On constant display, he made speeches and performed a little act on the stage. He learned to use the right knife and fork at dinner parties.

Like many star athletes, he went to Hollywood and made a picture. In Jack's case, it was a number of pictures — a serial called *Daredevil Jack*. It was no better and no worse than a dozen other cheaply shot, quickly made serials. Even Jack admitted that he was no actor, but the money was more than satisfactory.

He posed for stills with Tom Mix, and boxed with Rudolph Valentino, the smoldering lover of the screen. "He's not a bad boxer, but he can't punch worth a hang," was Dempsey's comment about the former tango dancer.

Jack's show-biz friends included Paul Whiteman, Mabel Normand, Sylvia Sydney, Bert Lahr, Fred and Adele Astaire, Charlie Chaplin, Douglas Fairbanks and Al Jolson. He was on backslapping terms with Jimmy Walker — later to become Mayor of New York City — and newspaperman Arthur "Bugs" Baer.

Jack was photographed wherever he went. People who had refused to give him the right time of day before he was champion now roared at his jokes and paid attention when he talked seriously. A practical joker, Dempsey became adept at giving hotfoots to unsuspecting celebrities. He made the rounds of Hollywood and Broadway speakeasies — an illegal but highly fashionable activity — but stayed away from hard liquor. Wine made him sleepy, so he drank beer. He was in a New York speakeasy when it was raided, and spent a night in jail — along with some of the best-known entertainment and sporting figures in the country.

But the Willard fight money was gone and Jack's movie and stage money was being spent as fast as he made it, so Kearns got him a couple of fights. The first was with Billy Miske and was partly in the nature of a favor. Miske was dying of Bright's disease and needed money badly.

Jack tried to be merciful and end the fight quickly, but he did not land solidly until the third round. Then Miske went down and stayed down. The effort was worth it for Miske. Afterward he picked up the largest purse of his entire life — $25,000. For his part, Dempsey was well paid. He and Kearns split $55,000.

In December, 1920, Jack almost lost his title to Bill Brennan. Overconfident because he had knocked Brennan silly in 6 rounds two years before when he had been on a diet of pickles and potato chips, Dempsey got careless. He walked into a stiff left and took a series of blows to the head before he could regain his balance. In the second round Brennan, determined to pull the upset of the year, caught Jack on the chin with an explosive right. Dempsey's knees buckled but he grabbed hold of Brennan and did not go down. For 5 rounds after that, virtually out on his feet, Jack fought by instinct. Then, slumped on his stool before the seventh, he was astonished to find Kearns screaming at him.

"You're going to lose the title!" Kearns was shouting. He flung water into Jack's face from the sponge.

"What round is it?" Dempsey croaked, partly revived by Kearns's voice. Kearns told him.

Dempsey had only a hazy memory of the previous rounds.

"You've got to knock him out, Jack!" Kearns told him. "He's won every round!"

Jack gulped air as Kearns ducked under the ropes, then stood up for the bell and Kearns propelled him to the center of the ring. He shuffled forward slowly, trying to gather strength. Brennan, a stand-up fighter, threw two jabs and followed with a hard, chopping right hand that almost tore off Jack's left ear. Startled and knowing he was badly hurt, Dempsey backed away and touched the ear with his glove. Warm blood covered the side of his head. His ear seemed to be almost completely severed. He back-pedaled for two rounds, trying to protect his ear from another such blow.

In the eleventh round, he recovered enough strength to hit the advancing Brennan a hard left hook in the stomach — Jack's best punch of the fight. The crowd stood up and roared as Brennan doubled up, then fell into a clinch. This was the Dempsey they had paid to see. In the twelfth round, after the pair had exchanged jabs, Dempsey lunged forward from his crouch, feinted a left to the head, and then brought his arm down for a straight punch at Brennan's solar plexus. The blow was so hard that Dempsey's fist disappeared from sight. He quickly followed this with his Sunday punch, a fierce left hook to the ribs. Brennan's eyes glazed as he slowly sank to his knees, hardly able to breathe, and toppled over. To the immense relief of Kearns, the referee tolled ten over the inert challenger.

The pain of having his ear sewed up was eased by the size of the purse Jack got. It was $100,000 plus $8,000 for the sale of the motion-picture rights. He split it with Kearns.

"You sure had me worried," Kearns bellowed above the babel in the dressing room.

Jack, holding a compress to his ear, nodded happily.

The door was flung open and Brennan burst into the room, all smiles. "I thought I won it, you lucky stiff," he shouted, slapping Jack on the back. "I had you glassy-eyed."

"How did it feel when he caught you with that left hook?" a reporter asked Brennan.

"Hardest punch I was ever hit," Brennan said. He opened his robe to show a giant bruise on the right side of his body.

"Jack's a born killer," said Kearns delightedly.

Jack Dempsey was not exactly a born killer, but every event in his early life and his struggles to fill his stomach as a young man on the bum had seemed to direct him toward one end — becoming the world's best fighter. Not only was he placed in the position of having to rely on his fists to stay alive, but he actually enjoyed fighting. He liked the feel of his fists hitting something solid, and liked the head-to-head combat in the ring, where neither man could back down. It pleased him that he had enough power in his fists to flatten larger and heavier fighters. He was proud of his ability to take the severest punishment they could deal out and come back for more.

JACK DEMPSEY

As a youngster in the tiny town of Manassa, Colorado, Harry Dempsey (he had not then adopted the name Jack) fought after school the way most children would play marbles or baseball. His father, a small but tough man, encouraged him to fight. So did his hard-working mother. Once she read a book about the life of John L. Sullivan, the Boston Strong Boy.

"I want you to be a champion like the great John L.," she told her eleven-year-old son. It seemed the only way Dempsey could ever make money.

From this tender age, Jack was in serious training to become heavyweight champion of the world.

Under the supervision of his older brother Bernie, a professional boxer, Jack would spar with another brother, Johnny. Johnny was a year older, but Jack could hold his own — mainly because even at that age he showed a killer instinct. He would never back up, regardless of the punishment he took.

It was Bernie who got young Harry the name of Jack. A middleweight, Bernie took the name Jack Dempsey after a famous middleweight fighter of the 1880's, who was also known as the Nonpareil. Johnny Dempsey, when he fought professionally, also adopted the name. Later Jack, who fought for a while as Kid Blackie (because of his dark complexion, as much as his determined scowl), would take the name used by his brothers.

Bernie had a glass jaw and could not take a punch, but he was a good coach for his younger brothers. He taught them how to slip punches and put their weight behind jabs, hooks and uppercuts, how to throw punches in combinations. He helped them make heavy bags out of sawdust and rags, and stuff workmen's gloves with padding to protect their knuckles.

When Jack was eleven, Bernie had him chew gum from

147

pine trees to make his jaw tough. Even when Jack was champion of the world, mingling with socialites and movie stars, he found time to chew this terrible-tasting resinlike gum.

Bernie also knew about the danger of cuts on a fighter's face — how referees might stop a fight because of cuts, and how a fighter's vision might be hindered because of a cut around his eye. Three times a day, he had Jack bathe his face in pails of beef brine obtained free from the butcher. Jack hated the smelly stuff, but he realized that soaking his face was good for it. This habit, too, he continued long after he was champion.

Jack Dempsey came by his fighting instinct naturally. His father, Hyrum, was a descendant of Irish immigrants who had settled in the tough coal-mining country of West Virginia. Both Hyrum Dempsey and his wife Celia were part Indian — Cherokee. Dempsey recalls his mother as the most magnificent woman he ever met, and the most courageous.

Hyrum was tall and wiry, a good hunter and fisherman, and loved the outdoors. His father had been a blacksmith and a champion wrestler. But in the small town of Mud Fork, he made his money as a schoolteacher — a job he despised.

One day a Mormon missionary stopping by the Dempsey house suggested that the Dempseys move to Colorado. The hunting and fishing were good there, he said, and the land was fertile. Also, lumber for building a ranchhouse was plentiful. Hyrum was only too happy to forsake teaching and take a chance. Celia felt the move might be good for the children. So the family — then consisting of Bernie and a sister — packed their meager belongings and made the long, wearying trek to Colorado in a prairie wagon. Unfortunately, the frontier town of Manassa, where Hyrum settled, had little to offer the Dempseys. Farmland was scarce, and the mines were too far away for Hyrum to work in them. If it had not been for the kindliness of their Mormon neighbors, the Dempseys would have starved.

William Harrison Dempsey was born in Manassa on June 24, 1895. The ninth of eleven children, he showed his Indian ancestry in his heavy black brows and hair. Growing up, he became a good, skillful and patient hunter and fisherman. This was lucky because the day's catch would often be the only food in the house.

The family had the habit of picking up and moving every year or so, looking for richer soil to plant in or settling near silver mines where the Dempsey males who were old enough grabbed a pick or shovel and went to work.

Jack's formal education was skimpy. Having more important problems, he did not take to books. When he was fourteen, he quit school entirely. "Harry Dempsey," cried the teacher one day, "you're the biggest, dumbest kid in school. Maybe you'd better leave." So Jack left and became a silver miner for a while — which he liked a lot better.

An incident that took place when Jack was very young gave him insight into the value of money. He and his younger brother Bruce were with their mother on the train going from Leadville, Colorado, to Denver. Celia had not been feeling well and her husband had urged her to stay with her sister for a few weeks.

The conductor came by, asking for tickets. Celia presented hers, but thought that Harry and Bruce were small enough to travel for nothing. The conductor insisted that she pay half fare for Harry.

"Or he'll have to get off at the next station," he announced solemnly. He was not sympathetic when Celia showed him her purse containing only a few coins. Promising to return, he walked down the aisle.

Jack was panic-stricken at the thought of being put off the train. All three members of the family were close to tears when he was surprised to find his sleeve tugged by a cowboy in a large hat.

"Tell your mother not to worry," the cowboy said in a low voice. "If the conductor comes back and asks for money, I'll pay your fare." He smiled encouragingly. Too choked up to voice his thanks, Jack ran to his mother and blurted out the good news. Then, as he stared out the window and watched tumbleweeds and scrubby trees rush by, he resolved — with all the fierceness an eight-year-old can muster — that he would never be poor and frightened like that again. Nothing was as bad as not having money.

When Jack was sixteen, like all the male Dempseys, he ran away from home. There simply was no way for the family to feed him, and he could not find work. He rode the rails from town to town, taking any job that was open. He shined shoes, picked fruit, acted as a porter in a hotel, cut firewood, scrubbed floors, mined silver. When no jobs were to be had, he hustled suckers in pool games and bowling contests. Oddly enough, he learned his bob-and-weave style of fighting from tossing large beets off railroad cars into farmers' wagons. To keep his balance while standing on the unsteady pile of beets, he had to bend his knees and crouch, rapidly shifting his weight from one side to the other. When he began to fight professionally, the crouch — a very tiring position unless you were used to it — became second nature to him.

Since riding the freights was against the law, he had many skirmishes with railroad yardmen. Once he was nearly killed. He had seized hold of a freight car ladder and was preparing to climb to the top when a burly brakeman appeared above his head.

"Get off, ya bum!" the brakeman shouted. He knelt down on the car roof so that he could reach Jack with his club.

Jack was afraid to let go because the train was going so fast. He would have been better off if he had jumped. The brakeman kept hitting him on top of the head until Jack was so groggy his fingers could no longer hold the ladder. Off he fell, hitting the cinders with terrific force, rolling over and over as the train roared ahead. A half-hour later, when he could get his legs under him, he limped forty miles to the next town, wondering how he was going to feed himself.

It was a rough, humbling life. When things got really desperate, Dempsey invented a novel way to make money. He would walk into a saloon as soon as it opened for the day and ask the bartender if any of his patrons were especially disliked. If the bartender had someone in mind and did not object to a fight being staged, Jack would hang around until the man came in. Then he would pick a fight with him. Because he was a skinny kid with a half-shaven head, a broken nose and scars on his face and wore beat-up shoes and an old torn sweater, many bartenders wanted no part of the arrangement. But some allowed him to pick his fight. After he had won (which he usually did), a collection would be taken up — Jack's reward for having knocked out an unpopular character. The bartender would keep half.

In towns where bartenders were quite hostile, Jack would sometimes strut into a filled saloon, bang his fist down on the bar, and announce, "I'm tough enough to lick anybody here." The temper of the times was such that he seldom failed to find a challenger — and he did not look as though he could stand up to burly miners and lean cowpokes whose main recreations were drinking and brawling. Obviously a callow kid, with his high-pitched voice, torn clothes and underfed appearance, Jack had no trouble getting saloon fights. After he had knocked his man out by the quickest method possible, the hat would be passed. Dempsey would pocket the coins and bills, down a few beers, send some money off to his mother and make his way to another town and another saloon.

When he needed time to recuperate from a pounding, or when business was slow, Jack would visit a local pool room, pretend to be a poor player until he could inveigle someone into a game for money, and then show his real skill.

It was in booming Salt Lake City that Dempsey first fought in the ring as a professional. A promoter named Harry Downey offered him $2.50 to take on a fighter named One-Punch Hancock. Dempsey, a decided underdog, knocked out Hancock with one punch.

"I see where he got the name," Dempsey smirked after the fight. But the promoter was furious.

"That was no fight!" He hurled at Dempsey, who was ready to step out of the ring. He was not even breathing hard.

"I can't pull my punches," Dempsey told him. "Call up somebody from the audience. But I want another two and a half bucks."

Downey, about to step inside the ropes, nodded. He got the crowd's attention and bawled over the noise that Kid Blackie would fight anyone in the audience for a purse of $2.50. A huge man stepped forward, calling Dempsey a lucky puncher. He was whisked to a dressing room and outfitted with trunks, gloves and a pair of shoes. It turned out that he was One-Punch's brother. Dempsey rushed forward, feinted with a right, then hooked with his left, first to the ribs and then to the chin, knocking Hancock out with two punches. It was an auspicious start.

During this often grim but lively period of his life Dempsey had good times and bad. Once he got the amazing sum of $20 for a bout. Once a local sheriff piously insisted that he wrestle his opponent instead of boxing him. Boxing was illegal, the sheriff pointed out. He failed to point out that Dempsey's opponent was a wrestling champion. It was either wrestle or go to jail, so Dempsey wrestled and took a terrible beating.

In the wild mining town of Goldfield, Nevada, Dempsey took another terrible beating — this time from a boxer, Johnny Sudenberg. After he was knocked out, Dempsey was dumped into a wheelbarrow and carted to his home — a cave in the side of a hill. He slept for twenty hours, then went to collect his money. Hungry, battered and sore, he learned that the man who had lined up the fight for him had run out of town with his money. It was the blackest day of Kid Blackie's life.

His ambition to become heavyweight champion of the world stayed with him, however. In Salt Lake City again, he built a low cage, ring-size but only four feet high. It was to enable him to perfect his crouch. He shadowboxed inside it until his back ached. If he straightened up while training, he got a bad bump on the head.

One day in the fall of 1914, while he performed his painful drill, Jack got the news that his brother Bernie was about to fight in Denver. Dempsey hopped the first freight heading that way, to give his brother whatever help and encouragement he could.

It developed that he was to do more than that. Bernie's opponent, George Copelin, was a hard, dogged puncher and very tough to knock off his feet. Bernie, nearing forty, knew it.

"I can't stand the altitude in this place," he confided to Jack in his small hotel room. "It's impossible for me to breathe when I get tired."

Jack had an idea. "Why don't I fight him?" he asked.

Bernie was willing, but the promoter, when he learned about the switch, was unhappy.

"This kid don't weigh but a hundred and forty pounds," he pointed out.

"A hundred and sixty," corrected Dempsey. "I'll fight under the same name as Bernie," he said. "The crowd'll never know."

Copelin was sent for. "I'll kill him," he announced when he saw the skinny, ravaged appearance of the substitute.

"Put your money where your mouth is," said the cocky Jack. He was willing to bet his end of the purse that he could flatten Copelin. That convinced the promoter, and Copelin was willing to settle for what he thought would be an easier opponent.

He was introduced as Jack Dempsey and the crowd soundly booed him, mainly because he looked so skinny compared to the husky Copelin. But the punk could throw a punch and he didn't mind getting hit. In between wild first-round exchanges which found the fighters slugging toe-to-toe, Dempsey floored Copelin six times. In the second round Copelin fell down twice. But the thin air of Denver was getting to Jack. He had trouble getting his breath when the second round ended. He stopped punching hard and concentrated on saving his strength. By the end of the sixth round, his lungs were on fire and he was ready to quit.

"Stick it out one more round, Harry," Bernie implored. "Copelin is worse off than you are." Across the ring, Copelin sat, his chest heaving, his mouth open with the effort of sucking air into his lungs.

"Just one more," Jack muttered when Bernie hoisted him to his feet and propelled him toward the center of the ring. Summoning all his reserves, Dempsey threw several round-house rights and lefts, all of which landed. Copelin was too weary to move or duck. Mercifully, the referee stopped the bout, and Jack was awarded a technical knockout. Bernie and his exhausted brother split the $100 purse.

"You learned to fight real good," Bernie commented, grateful that Harry had saved him from a bad beating.

Bernie went back to coal-mining and Harry — thereafter to be known in fighting circles as Jack — resumed his saloon fighting. When that failed to pay off, he continued to do any kind of work to make a dollar. Once in a while he managed to scrounge fights — always against bigger opponents. Finally, in Ely, Nevada, he met the man who was later to change his entire life.

In this out-of-the-way mining town, Jack fought a good heavyweight named Joe Bond who was managed by Jack "Doc" Kearns, a dapper, smooth-talking man with great ambitions. Kearns saw Jack lick his man in a hard, well-fought bout and congratulated him on his ability to punch and take a punch. He noticed that the wiry Dempsey had some growing to do. Afterward, when Dempsey's fortunes were at their lowest, Kearns was to remember how Dempsey had managed to tag the elusive Bond and would stake his future on Jack.

Feeling elated over this victory, Dempsey took a giant step and invaded New York City, where the big money was supposed to be. He did not look like a prosperous fighter to the sophisticated citizens of New York — a shabby young man who had to shave every four hours. He carried a cardboard suitcase and spoke with an accent Easterners found difficult to understand.

He had one suit of clothes. Nobody had ever heard of him, and no manager was willing to take him on. No promoter would give him a fight. He starved. He gave up his dingy hotel room and lived in the park. Finally he got a fight with a huge heavyweight named André Anderson.

Because of his lack of funds, Dempsey's training methods were unique. He would go into a bar and grab the beer of a half-drunk patron. Then, flourishing the mug like a big spender, he would amble to the free-lunch counter and gobble down as much food as he could hold. While chewing, he would stuff his pockets with good things for lean days to come. Whatever flesh he put on, he tried to work off by running in the park and sparring in an uptown gym.

He weighed only 162 when he fought Anderson, who was strong and tried to bull Dempsey all around the ring. Jack took a shellacking for 3 rounds, then recuperated enough to land some solid shots in the next 5. No decision was awarded by the referees, but the papers gave the fight to Dempsey. He got $20 for his cuts and bruises.

After Jack had whipped a fighter called Wild Bert Kennedy, a wicked fate threw him into the hands of John the Barber Reisler. In return for lining up a fight for the desperate Dempsey, Reisler appointed himself Jack's manager. The fight was with John Lester Johnson — a sinewy Negro who had beaten the formidable Gunboat Smith and had even won a decision over the great Sam Langford. (Langford was so dangerous a fighter that the heavyweight champion, Jack Johnson, refused to meet him in the ring.)

John Lester Johnson gave Jack the worst beating of his life — worse than Sudenberg, worse than the railroad brakeman. In the second round, Johnson hit Jack the hardest blow he was ever struck — a right-hand hook to the body that caved in three of Jack's ribs. The pain was agonizing. For the next few rounds Jack was panicky lest Johnson hit him there again and drive a broken rib through his lungs or heart.

But as the fight wore on, Jack's amazing powers of recuperation took over and he was able to throw some punches of his own. When the last round ended with both men on their feet, Johnson seemed to be suffering almost as much as Jack. A few newspaper writers awarded Jack the bout, but most of them said Johnson had won. Dempsey himself would have given it to Johnson by a mile. The $35 he got, after Reisler's cut, was hardly enough to pay for bandages, tape, salve and disinfectant.

Taped up so that he could hardly breathe, aching in every joint, sporting a pair of shiners, Jack was thoroughly discouraged about the fight game. Without thanking John the Barber, he left town and rode the rails to Salt Lake City, where his mother had now set up a home.

He worked in a copper mine for a while, then was lured back into the ring for a gigantic purse of $250. He won by a 3-round knockout. He gave his mother half the money, and once more filled with optimism, returned to New York. This time he rode in style.

John the Barber promptly offered him a fight with Sam Langford, but Jack, not wishing to die in the ring, turned it down. Unable to get any other fight, he hopped a freight and found himself, several nights later, in Kansas City. There, learning that the tall, strong Carl Morris was in training for a fight with Frank Moran, Jack got himself hired as a willing punching bag for Morris. He got 75¢ a day.

The experience held one pleasant surprise. Sparring with

Morris one afternoon in the gym, Jack realized that, with his speed, toughness and hitting power, he could beat Morris — and Morris, called the Sepulpa Giant, was a top heavyweight contender. When the fight between Morris and Moran was postponed (because Moran had hurt his hand), Jack begged to be allowed to substitute. But the promoter decided Jack's reputation was not big enough.

"If he whips you, what good will it do him?" the promoter asked. "And if you should happen to beat him, he might lose his shot at Johnson."

Jack quit the training camp and accepted the hospitality of another freight car. This time he got off at Pueblo, Colorado. Staying for a day in a hobo jungle there — where he could be assured of a meal if he contributed something to the stewpot — he was arrested for a peculiar reason. The local politicians were having a bowling tournament, and hobos were being pressed into service as pin boys. When a ball was dropped on Jack's hand by an amateur pin setter, the cops let him go, and he hastened out of town.

In Pueblo, Colorado, he was unlucky enough to land a fight with Fireman Jim Flynn, another of the country's white hopes. Flynn was extremely tough, rated on a par with Gunboat Smith, and Jack was knocked out in two rounds — or as good as knocked out. Bernie had come to Pueblo to act as Jack's second. After Jack had been knocked down four times, Bernie threw in the towel and the referee awarded the fight to Flynn.

"Why'd you stop it?" Jack murmured through puffed lips when he realized the fight was over.

"Because he was knocking you all around the ring," Bernie told him.

Ruefully, Jack admitted his brother was right.

Discouraged by the lumps he had taken from Flynn, Jack

called it a day after five years of trying to make a living as a professional fighter. He journeyed up to Seattle to work for several months as a lumberjack, then returned to Salt Lake City, ready to take any kind of a job he could get. If, after a few weeks at home, he had not received a telegram from Doc Kearns, boxing history would have taken a different course.

Kearns wanted to know if Jack was still fighting. Amazed that the shrewd manager should be interested in a broken-down young pug like himself, Jack wrote back that he would be happy to fight anyone Kearns could line up for him. Kearns astonished him even more by sending him a train ticket to Los Angeles, where the manager lived, and a $5 bill. This showed that Kearns had class.

Kearns saw to it that Jack ate well, had good sparring partners, and trained hard. Jack fought a few good bouts against unknowns, winning them all, then Kearns presented him with the acid test — a fight with Gunboat Smith in San Francisco.

Aware of Smith's punching power, the lighter Dempsey kept away from him in the first round. But he got momentarily careless in the second and was on the receiving end of a pile-driver straight right that almost took his head off his shoulders. Groggy, Dempsey lasted out the round and wandered to his corner, waggling his chin, which seemed to have come loose. The punch to his jaw was the last thing he remembered. He came to his senses hours after the fight was over. He was looking over the rail of a ferryboat returning to Oakland.

Noticing Kearns beside him, staring down at the black water below, Jack apologized for getting knocked out.

"I'm sorry I lost, Doc," he mumbled to Kearns. He was not good at apologies.

159

"What do you mean?" demanded the astounded Kearns. He thought Jack was kidding, then realized he was dead serious. "You licked him! By a knockout!"

Finally Jack figured out what happened. After the second round, he had fought the rest of the fight in a complete blackout. His training, instinct and will to win had carried him through.

Kearns slapped Jack on the back. He was proud of this tough young man who had overcome so much adversity to get where he finally was. "You got him with body punches, Jack. You're going to be heavyweight champion of the world."

Three successive fights with gigantic Carl Morris were next for Dempsey, and he won all three. The last bout took less than one minute. Jack's years of apprenticeship in saloons, his baths in brine, and his practice inside the cage, were paying off. In another fight, he hit Bill Brennan so hard that, in falling, Brennan broke his ankle, ending the fight. After beating Billy Miske twice, Jack was offered a fight by the manager of experienced Fred Fulton.

Neither Fulton nor his manager took Dempsey seriously. "How can a kid his size have a punch?" they asked one another.

Fulton was rangy and fast. He jabbed well and counter-punched with a fast right. He was one of the few fighters to hold a decision over Sam Langford.

"Beat this guy," murmured Kearns into Jack's ear in the corner before the bell rang, "and your next opponent has got to be Willard."

Dempsey sprang forward in his crouch, weaving from his hips, his head bobbing up and down — an elusive target. He waited for Fulton to present his chin, and then chopped at it with a hard right. Fulton toppled over in eight seconds of the first round and stayed down long after the count of ten.

Kearns was right. Though he was the youngest, smallest and least-known of all the challengers, Dempsey was picked to fight Willard.

The two most important men in Jack Dempsey's life were Doc Kearns, with whom he later broke, and George L. "Tex" Rickard, the boxing promoter. "Fighting isn't fun anymore," Dempsey said after Rickard's funeral in 1929. It was Rickard's genius for publicizing and dramatizing fights, as well as Dempsey's appeal to the fans, that resulted in the fabulous prizefight gates of the Twenties.

Like Kearns and Dempsey, Rickard was a product of the rough, no-holds-barred West. If anything, he pursued an even more checkered career than the other two. He was an instinctive gambler, generous with his friends, and a picturesque adventurer. He could act tough when he had to, but he was known for never going back on his word.

Rickard had been introduced to violence in his early years. Frank and Jesse James happened to live next door to the Rickard cabin in Kansas City, Missouri. When Tex was ten, he saw a hard-riding posse come gunning after the outlaw brothers. At the age of eleven, he became a wrangler, spending long days in the saddle, riding herd on a rancher's cattle. When he was twenty, he became marshal of a nervous town on the Texas border. From there he migrated to the Yukon, making a living as a dealer in the gambling houses that sprang up wherever gold and silver strikes were made. When the Klondike Gold Rush started in 1895, Tex joined the scramble for gold, making fortunes by prospecting, losing fortunes by gambling. Returning to the other side of the table, Rickard operated a gambling saloon in Nome — the only honest one in Alaska, his claim went. When his customers' gold ran out, he operated one in Goldfield, Nevada. He became involved in other pursuits — seeking a diamond mine in South Africa, and spending five years in Paraguay running a 5,000,000-acre ranch.

Rickard got into boxing — still another form of gambling — in an odd way. While in Goldfield, he tried to sell some copper properties to a rich prospector.

"Copper doesn't interest me," said the prospector over his whiskey. "What I'd like to see is a fight between Jack Johnson and Jim Jeffries in Reno. Put Reno on the map. If you promote it, I'll furnish the money."

Johnson was the heavyweight champion, and Jeffries was the retired former champion. The enthusiasm of many white fans had been aroused for this fight, since no other white man seemed to have a chance against Johnson. Jeffries, though thirty-five years old and twenty pounds overweight, was a last hope, as well as a white hope.

"You've got yourself a deal," Tex told the prospector, and they shook on it.

There was the inevitable competition from other promoters, but Tex confounded his rivals by offering $101,000 to stage the fight. To substantiate the claim, he plunked down a bag containing $20,000 in gold in front of Jeffries. This lured the former champion out of retirement and settled doubts that there would be a fight and that Tex could meet his guarantees.

A dispute about the referee was solved by Tex — he refereed himself. The bout was a one-sided one, with Johnson methodically cutting his older rival to pieces, but financially it made boxing history. Gate receipts came to almost $271,000, the largest up to that time. If one had foresight and was willing to take a long chance, Tex reasoned, this was a splendid way to make money.

Two years after Dempsey beat Willard and had seemingly run out of opponents, Rickard came up with the perfect opponent — perfect, that is, from the standpoint of drama. The opponent was Georges Carpentier of France. Carpentier had been a war hero (which Dempsey was not) and had the distinction of having won every weight championship of his country as he progressed in size and boxing skill. He was also the European heavyweight champion. Unfortunately, he was not quite 170 pounds.

Rickard's sense of showmanship, after the fight had been arranged, led him to paint Dempsey as a villain for this bout and Carpentier as a hero. Dempsey was glowering, unshaven, a step away from the hobo jungles; Carpentier, by contrast, was publicized as a gentleman, an ace whose wartime feats were cited daily in the press and a student of culture. Dempsey's training camp was filled with hangers-on and rowdies. The handsome, courteous Carpentier trained on Long Island and spent most of his time with society folk.

Dempsey's training ritual was open to the public, but guards and barbed wire kept visitors and reporters away from Carpentier's camp. The Frenchman's manager explained that his fighter was developing a secret punch to flatten Dempsey. The fact was, reporters were kept away for fear that they would reveal that Carpentier was too small a man to put up much of a struggle against the killer.

To accommodate the thousands of fans expected for the fight, Rickard had a huge arena built at Boyle's Thirty Acres in Jersey City. Everything pointed to a record attendance, but Kearns, when he was offered a choice between a flat $300,000 or a percentage of the gate, unwisely chose the former. This decision — which cost him $75,000 and Jack an equal amount — started the friction between Kearns and Rickard.

The fight was scheduled to start at three in the afternoon on July 2, 1921. But at one o'clock the local fire chief and police chief burst into Dempsey's hotel room.

"Let's get moving, Jack," the police chief urged. He wore a troubled look. "The fight has to go on early. The arena Tex built is beginning to sway back and forth. Rickard wants the fight to start before it collapses."

Rickard greeted Jack at the side entrance. He seemed less worried about a swaying arena than elated over the size and quality of the crowd. "Wait'll you see the swells and classy dames who bought tickets." He chortled. "For the first time, boxing is respectable."

In Jack's dressing room he became more serious. "Listen, Jack," he said. "This is the biggest day in boxing history. And there can be dozens more paydays just as big."

"So?" Dempsey was puzzled.

"So don't spoil it for everybody," Tex blurted, "by killing this Frenchman. Kill him, and you kill boxing." Rickard's sense of drama extended to his speech.

Dempsey scowled at his friend and spoke curtly. "I'm not going to take it easy on him for you or anybody," he said. "Now let me get dressed."

As champion, Dempsey was introduced first. There were a few cheers but these were quickly drowned out by boos and catcalls. The anti-Dempsey sentiment was occasioned by a comparison of the war records of the two fighters — a comparison that had been hammered into the minds of the fans for several months. Most of them, however, were unaware of the true story about Dempsey and the draft board.

During the war, Dempsey had been granted a deferment by the board because he was supporting his father and mother. But because he had made an enemy of a sports editor who claimed that Dempsey's claims were false, Dempsey was brought to trial on these charges before a grand jury in 1920. In an unpleasant five-day trial, accusations were aired and witnesses testified. It took the jury only fifteen minutes to acquit the champion, but the unjust charge of "Slacker" stuck. The average man on the street felt it unjust that a man as healthy and strong as Dempsey should stay home while less athletic citizens fought in the trenches. Afterward, whenever Dempsey took a stroll or fought or appeared on the stage, he was apt to have the epithet hurled at him. That it was unjust did not lessen the cut inflicted. And the chorus of boos at Boyle's Thirty Acres hurt even more.

Cheers, applause and the stamping of feet shook the arena when the smiling, confident Carpentier was introduced. However, charm is no substitute for ruggedness in the prize ring, and those who had counted on him to dethrone the champion were a little dismayed by his relatively slender appearance.

On Kearn's advice, Dempsey was cautious in the first round, staying away from Carpentier's vaunted straight right. Carpentier boxed skillfully, making Dempsey seem a plodder by comparison, but neither fighter landed an effective blow. As Dempsey returned to his corner, someone called him a slacker.

"You bum!" someone else shouted.

In the second round, Carpentier brought the fans screaming to their feet. He smashed Dempsey in the head with a right that seemed to have come from nowhere. But it hit Jack high on his left cheekbone. Dempsey did not go down, but he was staggered and could not defend himself properly. Following up his advantage, Carpentier kept pouring lefts and rights to Jack's head. His back against the ropes, Jack absorbed everything thrown at him. Then, seeing an opening, he shot a short, hard right to Carpentier's mouth.

Instantly, Jack knew that the fight was his. Carpentier could sting him but not knock him out. From the surprised, anguished look on Carpentier's face, Jack knew he had never been hit so hard before by a punch that had traveled so short a distance.

Kearns echoed Dempsey's confidence. "Shoot for his body," he ordered, rubbing the back of Jack's neck. "When his guard comes down, the left to his chin."

Dempsey nodded. But he had to stay away from the Frenchman's right.

All through the third round, Dempsey pounded away at Carpentier's ribs and stomach. In the fourth round, Carpentier lowered his hands to protect this vital area, but left his jaw open. Dempsey feinted with a right and hooked with a left that landed flush on the Frenchman's chin. He went down for a count of nine. As he rose, Dempsey glided in and struck Carpentier with a right to the heart and a left to the jaw. Carpentier could not rise, and the championship was secure. In a sincerely friendly gesture, Dempsey helped pick Carpentier up and carry him to his corner.

Reading the papers the next day, Jack was surprised to see that more space was given to Carpentier's skill and gentlemanliness than the critical events in the fourth round. Obviously the papers were still committed to the hero-villain aspect of the bout.

"You'd think the other guy had won the fight," Dempsey muttered, soaking off his bruises in a hot tub.

But Kearns was more intrigued with the figures. The gate had been $1,626,580 — the first time a fight had brought in over a million. Calculating with a pencil, Kearns figured out how much his mistake in not taking a percentage had cost him. He was not at all pleased about it.

Neither Doc nor Jack had paid any attention to a bout that had preceded the main event. In it, Sailor Jones had been defeated in a dull fight that had brought boos for its lack of action. The winner had been a former Marine named Gene Tunney.

Since no worthwhile opponents were around, Doc and Jack decided to take a junket to Europe. There Jack found himself lionized as a sports hero. He hobnobbed with an English prince who later was to become ruler of the Empire, and partied with generals, lords and dukes. In France, he was nearly mobbed at the Longchamps race track, refereed a bout in Paris, and received a medal from the French Government. In Germany, he made the mistake of telling reporters that he loved German sheep dogs. The next day a thousand owners of sheep dogs appeared at his hotel to press a dog on him, completely wrecking the lobby.

After more touring, night-clubbing and basking in admiration, funds became low. Kearns informed Jack that he would have to get back into training for a major fight, and they returned to America.

A major fight was hard to find. Meanwhile, Jack was slaughtering everyone with nerve enough to step in the ring with him — sometimes as many as three in a single night. Rickard still seemed unable to produce a worthwhile opponent.

Then came the Shelby fiasco. Having grown estranged from Rickard, Kearns jumped at the chance of involving Dempsey in a big fight without including the foremost promoter in America. The opportunity came when some citizens of Shelby, a small town in Montana, approached Kearns with an offer. It seemed that oil had been struck in Shelby, and to help the sale of oil stocks, they wanted to make the town famous. Holding a heavyweight championship fight there, they figured, was the quickest and surest way of doing it.

Dempsey had heard of his prospective opponent — Tommy Gibbons, an expert boxer — but had doubts about the location.

"Shelby?" he said to Kearns. "I never heard of it."

When he was told that he would get $100,000 on signing, an equal amount thirty days before the fight and $10,000 ten days before, he swallowed his misgivings. As usual, even in those days of tiny income taxes, Kearns could use the money.

It was an extremely confused project run by promoters with none of Rickard's experience. Dempsey received his money on signing, but thirty days before the fight it did not look as though the rest would be forthcoming. A frantic passing of the hat in Shelby raised the second payment. Kearns, noting the difficulty the citizens had in meeting their guarantees, waived the final payment, saying he would take it out of the gate.

But the gate did not furnish it. So badly managed was the crowd that half pushed their way in without paying. During the preliminary bouts, whooping fans tossed lariats around the fences and pulled them down, allowing more spectators to stream in. Holders of tickets found themselves standing outside the arena. Dempsey's special bodyguard, who carried two revolvers in case of trouble, was so frightened by the unruly fans that he scampered under the ring and hid there.

Not having fought a serious bout in two years, Dempsey was rusty. This circumstance, plus Gibbons' skill and determination not to get knocked out, made for a dull fight. Tommy would jab and run away; Jack never could set him up for a solid punch. After the referee awarded Jack the decision for aggressiveness, the champion and Kearns scooted out of town as fast as possible, taking their loot with them. As things turned out, they were the only ones to get anything out of the fight.

Gibbons, who was supposed to receive a share of the gate, got nothing. The investors got nothing. Shelby, instead of becoming famous, was nearly wiped off the map. Three banks failed. The rich men of the town were broke, no buying boom developed, and all the promoters were pestered long afterward for money they owed. It was a lesson in how not to put on a championship fight.

Jack's popularity sank to a new low after the Shelby affair, but in some ways that fight helped his career. It showed him that he had to work hard to get in shape. It convinced fans that he was not the invincible Mauler he used to be — and that his title could be taken away from him. Shrewdly, Rickard counted on this anticipation to furnish another huge championship gate. And meanwhile, Gene Tunney took satisfaction in noting that the Dempsey who could slaughter big, slow men made a poor showing against a skillful boxer. He stepped up his training for the showdown he was sure would come.

Again Rickard produced an opponent for Jack who was a box-office natural. This was Luis Angel Firpo of Argentina, a large, savage, shaggy man with soulful eyes. Firpo, who was six feet three and weighed 220 pounds, was advertised as the heavyweight champion of South America. That he could punch like a mule and take a punch was proven by his knockout of Bill Brennan. Then he flattened Jess Willard, who had been trying to make a comeback.

Rickard saw Firpo as a wild creature from an exotic land who was sure to capture the enthusiasm of the fans — most of whom would not have been unhappy if Dempsey had been slugged to insensibility.

Firpo, a stubborn man, did not improve his chances of

beating Dempsey by his training methods: he ate huge meals, fired his very competent American trainer, and refused to do roadwork. For his peace of mind, he surrounded himself with yes-men from his own country.

Aware of Firpo's preparations for the fight, Rickard paid a visit to Dempsey's dressing room before the main event — it was getting to be a habit.

"We got over a million-dollar gate here, Jack," said Tex earnestly. "Ninety thousand wild customers. They expect a fight. Give them a run for their money." Tex feared a reaction if Dempsey should knock out the South American champion with one punch.

But, as usual, Dempsey was having none of it. Firpo was a much more dangerous opponent than Carpentier.

"He could take me out with one punch, Tex," Jack said. "I'm going to flatten him as fast as I can."

Dempsey set out to do just that. At the bell, he charged to the center of the ring, bobbing, weaving, feinting and probing with his left. After straightening Firpo up with a hard jab, Jack thought he saw an opening for his right, and swung. Firpo rolled with the punch and countered with a roundhouse left that caught Dempsey high on the cheekbone. Not only did Jack tumble to the canvas, but he was rendered senseless for the entire round.

As in the Gunboat Smith fight, Jack carried on by instinct. Up at the count of six, he hooked with a left and threw an overhand right. Now it was Firpo who was on the canvas. The crowd, screaming for a knockout by Firpo, yelled encouragement to the Argentinean as he rested on one knee.

Through a haze, Dempsey saw Firpo climb to his feet. Rushing forward, Jack hit him twice in the head, and down went Luis for the second time. Again he rose, only to be slammed down. This happened four more times. The crowd, standing on seats, leaping up and down in the aisles, was approaching hysteria.

Then, with a little over ten seconds left in the round, Firpo gamely tore at Jack, arms wildly swinging. Dempsey backed away from the onslaught, trying to fend off the punches. Firpo hit Jack in the face with a blind right-hand swing, and Dempsey crashed through the ropes. He landed on the typewriter of one of the ringside sportswriters, completely smashing it.

The noise of the crowd was deafening. Not only had Firpo soaked up enough leather to fell a dozen heavyweights, but he was on the verge of capturing Dempsey's title! In deep trouble, Dempsey got a break when several sportswriters helped hoist him back into the ring. Later, he said he remembered nothing of being knocked out of the ring or being pushed back in.

A weary Firpo awaited him. Dempsey hurled himself across the ring and managed to land a hard punch to Firpo's heart before the bell clanged. Thus ended the most exciting round in the history of boxing.

Sitting on his stool, Dempsey heard angry voices.

"Where are the smelling salts?" someone asked.

"You had 'em," someone snapped.

Somebody slapped Dempsey's face. He felt a full sting.
"Here they are."

Jack recoiled as the pungent smell of the salts attacked his nostrils. Kearns had found the bottle in his shirt pocket.

Dempsey tried to recover his voice. "What round did he get me in?" he asked, trying to bring Kearns into focus.

"He knocked you through the ropes, that's all!" Kearns shouted. "Second round's coming up."

A great wave of relief swept through Dempsey. There was a chance to save the title!

When the bell rang, he darted from his corner, tense, aroused, eager to slam home punches. He raked Firpo with lefts and rights to the body. Firpo countered with a hard right that hurt Dempsey's ribs. Jack moved into a clinch to get his breath. When they were separated, he threw two short but damaging hooks to Firpo's body, then shot home a right uppercut to the jaw. He could see that Firpo was slowing down. Cornered by the ropes, Firpo tried to seize Jack's arms, but Jack burst loose. Two short, rapid-fire shots to the body and a left hook that dug into the Argentinean's ribs — the power of the blows sent Firpo crumbling to the canvas. Dazed and defenseless, he rose at five, only to be peppered by jabs and hooks to his head. Like a panther, Dempsey glided forward and smashed a right to Firpo's jaw.

Firpo swayed and went down. Breathing heavily, his arms leaden and his legs numb, Dempsey leaned against the ropes, hoping that the South American giant would not rise. For a count of six Firpo lay motionless on his face. Then he started to twist on the canvas and rolled over on his back. But this time he could not haul himself to his feet. For the second time, Dempsey's magnificent will to keep fighting had earned him a victory.

Like many heavyweight champions before and since, Dempsey seemed to have run out of worthwhile opponents. He took advantage of the lull by visiting Hollywood, consorting with the royalty of the movie colony and undergoing an operation that changed his much-battered nose into one more streamlined and handsome. Introduced to the beautiful and witty motion-picture star Estelle Taylor, Dempsey surprised his friends by courting and marrying her in 1925.

For critics who smirked that she was hurting her career by marrying a prizefighter, Estelle had a ready answer: "I'm not marrying a fighter," she said, "I'm marrying a champion."

During their honeymoon trip to Europe, Jack kept in shape by boxing European hopefuls, and Estelle became enamored of a huge hound which they brought back to America with them. Then, to the astonishment of the fistic world, Jack consented to take a part in a Broadway play. He would probably not have taken a flier at the theatre except that his wife was to play opposite him.

But Jack was no actor. Conscious of his high-pitched voice, never at home in the artificial stage world, Jack spent miserable hours trying to master a role that should have been easy for him. In a drama called *The Big Fight*, Jack played the part of Tiger, a fighter who had risen from squalid surroundings, punched his way to a title, and won the girl. Except for a fight scene in the last act, the play was terrible, and everybody knew it.

The opponent Jack was supposed to knock out every night was a former fighter named Jack Smith. Smith was seven feet tall and weighed 280 pounds, but he knew how to go down under Dempsey's punches.

One night in New Haven, during the play's tryout, Dempsey landed his usual haymaker right and waited for Smith to come crashing down, shaking the theatre. Instead, Smith countered with a hard right to Dempsey's jaw. A frenzied stage manager clanged the bell, and a groggy Dempsey was led back to his corner. For two more rounds, Dempsey carefully pulled his punches, hoping that Smith would revert to the script.

"What are you trying to do?" he demanded of Smith during one of their clinches.

Smith's answer was to break loose and try to fell Jack with a looping left. That settled it for the champion. He went after Smith for real, landing two punches — a left to the ribs and a right to the jaw. Smith went down and out. Later, in the dressing room, an upset Dempsey got the explanation. One of his first-round punches had knocked Smith out, and from there on he had fought by instinct. Dempsey grinned and threw his arm around the giant. He knew the sensation.

"It happened to me against Firpo," he told Smith.

"And remember what happened to Firpo," Smith said ruefully, rubbing his jaw.

Thanks to the drawing power of Jack and Estelle, the play lasted on Broadway for six weeks. With Kearns continuing to take 50 percent of his earnings, Jack forsook the legitimate stage and went on a vaudeville tour. When this ended, he barnstormed with a circus, offering a $1,000 to anyone who could stay three rounds with him. There were many challengers, but no one ever won the money.

Meanwhile, Jack was becoming bitter over his treatment by Kearns. Not only was Kearns receiving a fantastic percentage of what Jack made, but he also seemed to handle most of the money — often failing to give Jack an accounting. Finally Jack got proof that Kearns was shortchanging him. For his part, Kearns did not like Jack's wife — his main objection being to her wisecracks.

A deal whereby Kearns sold something belonging to Jack without telling him was the last straw.

"I want out, Doc," Dempsey told him. "If you want to stay on as my manager, you'll receive a one-third cut. That's all you get."

Disturbed that the former hobo had become suspicious of his transactions, Kearns blew up. "I'll see that you never fight again," was his parting threat before he stormed out.

He promptly began a series of lawsuits against Jack that bothered Dempsey for years thereafter. One of them was thrown out of court when the judge discovered that Kearns had not filed an income tax return on money he had received from the Firpo fight.

Jack had not fought for three years, mainly because Rickard thought no fighter could capture the fans' fancy as a worthy opponent. But at last he discovered one. This was Gene Tunney, whom Rickard did not think highly of as a threat to Jack but who appealed to Tex's sense of drama.

For Gene, like Carpentier, was many things that Jack was not. Dempsey was an instinctive fighter; Gene was a careful student of boxing. Tunney had fought with the Marines; Dempsey was regarded as a slacker by many. Dempsey was extremely nervous before a fight; Tunney was the picture of calmness. Tunney was good-looking, with an open face, and he was articulate. He liked to read Shakespeare and engaged in thoughtful conversations with intellectual friends.

But beneath his cultured exterior, Tunney was a tough, determined competitor. Like Dempsey, he had been born poor — in New York's Greenwich Village — and developed ambitions to become rich. While in the Marines, he found he could escape the boredom of behind-the-lines soldiering in France by boxing. He applied himself and managed to win the light-heavyweight championship of the American Expeditionary Forces. Back in America, taking stock of his situation, he saw that the quickest way to riches was to become a boxing champion. Overcoming weaknesses in his knuckles and his left arm by tireless work, he carefully planned his route to the top. He did not escape unscathed, however.

In the only fight he lost as a professional — the first of four with the "human windmill," Harry Greb — Tunney suffered a broken nose, a badly cut mouth and a pair of black eyes.

"You really gave me a bad time out there," said Tunney's manager as Tunney was having some stitches taken under one eye. Tunney was in great pain, and his manager's lack of sympathy so angered him that he decided to buy back the man's contract. Afterward, Tunney won over Greb three successive times. Gene knew he was improving because each victory was more thorough.

Besides Greb, Tunney beat Kingfish Levinsky, the light-heavyweight champion, and knocked out Tommy Gibbons — whom Dempsey had been unable to flatten. Tunney was not a spectacular fighter, but his punches were punishing and calculated to wear his opponent down round by round. He was also one of the hardest men to hurt in the history of boxing, so good were his defenses. His battle plan for Dempsey was to let Jack do the leading and pursuing and counterpunch, particularly with his right.

And Dempsey's battle plan? He had none. For one thing, he took Tunney lightly, assuming he could break through any defense and land his devastating hooks. For another, he was too busy avoiding subpoena servers and testifying in court to worry about Tunney. On one occasion, to avoid being haled into court by Kearns, Jack had crashed through a beaverboard wall. Another time, Kearns had Estelle's ritzy Rolls-Royce seized while she was riding in it. The star had to get out and walk miles back to her hotel.

"Every time I hit a punching bag," Dempsey fretted, "one of Kearns's summonses drops out of it."

While most of the public and even Rickard thought Gene

would be easy pickings for Dempsey, Tunney calmly figured out Jack's weaknesses. Gene's coolness was shown by
his decision to fly from his training camp in Stroudsberg,
Pennsylvania, to Philadelphia, where the fight was to be
held. This was at a time when many people thought flying
suicidal. Rickard, who had many thousands of dollars invested in the bout, was one of them. He flew into a rage
when he heard about the flight.

As for Tunney, he was deathly sick on the short trip and
regretted his bravado in choosing this crazy means of trans-
portation. "Never again," he gasped as he forced a pallid
smile for the reporters gathered around the light plane.

It rained in Philadelphia on the night of September 23,
1926, but that did not keep the fans away from Sesquicen-
tennial Stadium, where Rickard staged the fight. Almost
121,000 showed up, paying $1,895,723, making this the
largest gate in boxing history. Jack's share — one third of
which went to his new manager, Leo Flynn — was $800,-
000. Although Jack was thirty-one years old and Tunney
was twenty-eight, the public, as usual, went for the slugger
against the boxer. The odds favored Dempsey 3–1.

Tunney, confident and in superb condition, settled the
outcome of the fight with the first punch in the first round.
As the bell clanged, he sprang forward from his corner and
hit Jack in the mouth with a hard, straight right.

Recoiling from the accurate blow, Dempsey thought, No
one ever did that to me before, and his poise was shaken.
The rest of the fight, for 10 rounds, consisted of Dempsey
chasing Tunney and Tunney making Dempsey miss. From
time to time, Gene would land hard blows of his own when
Jack found himself off balance. The wet ring seemed to
slow Jack down, but Gene was not affected by it.

As the fight wore on, it became more and more apparent

that Gene was the champion's master. He jabbed and hooked and ripped Dempsey whenever he wished. Jack's legs began to feel like lead and they refused to take him where he wanted to go.

At the final gong, Jack was dazed and exhausted. He went back to his corner to await the decision, knowing that he had lost the title.

"The winner," cried the announcer, "and *new* heavyweight champion of the world — Gene Tunney!"

The roar could have been heard for miles as the announcer held up the smiling Tunney's hand. Surprise was the cause for much of the bedlam, since many fans had thought Jack to be unconquerable. Programs were scaled, hats were flung, and cheers and applause rocked the arena.

Jack was now the old, defeated champion. He took a deep breath and walked over to Tunney's corner. He put his arm around the nearly unmarked ex-Marine and said, "Gene, I know you're going to be a great champion. Lots of luck to you."

As Dempsey returned to his corner, a robe thrown loosely around his shoulders, a curious thing happened. The fans began cheering for him — louder than they had ever cheered before and louder than they had cheered for Tunney. Tough as he thought he was, Dempsey felt a lump rise in his throat. The fans were *applauding* him.

An incident later that night served to increase this newfound affection the fans developed for Jack. At a press conference held at the Ritz Hotel, Estelle came over to him, put her arms around her defeated husband, and asked him, "What happened, Ginsburg?"

The pet name caused Dempsey to grin. "I forgot to duck, honey," he told her.

There was one happy note, however. An ex-champion

needs money, and the wily Rickard had been able to fool
Doc Kearns's lawyers, who had orders to tie up Jack's purse.
The day before the fight, Tex had filled a suitcase with
$711,686 in cash and had wired it to Jack's brother Joe in
California. Joe stuck the money in a bank vault, where
Doc's lawyers could not locate it.

But Tex was very disappointed by Jack's showing against
Tunney. Not only because of friendship but for business
reasons. The fans had been attracted by Dempsey. Tunney
did not appeal to their imagination.

Tex asked Jack about a return bout.

"I don't think so, Tex," said Jack. "It's hard for me to get
in condition. I took quite a walloping in that first fight, and
I'm not looking forward to another."

The only outstanding heavyweight around was an ex-
sailor named Jack Sharkey. Sharkey, a good boxer, had
beaten Harry Wills, a fine Negro heavyweight of the day.
But just about the time Rickard had decided on Sharkey as
a challenger, Dempsey became convinced that, with the
proper conditioning, he could do something that no heavyweight had ever done — regain his title. One of those who
helped convince him was William Muldoon, a New York
boxing commissioner. (Muldoon had trained John L. Sullivan for his victory over Jake Kilrain.)

"You were overconfident the last time," he told Jack.
"You were rusty. You had worries. No wonder you lost."

His feelings were echoed by many of Jack's friends —
and hosts of new admirers who suddenly felt affection for
the down-to-earth ex-champion.

On Muldoon's advice, Jack spent three rugged months in
the mountains, running, shadowboxing and chopping down
trees. He worked as hard as he had almost ten years before
for the Willard fight. Rickard, however, was dubious about

Jack's ability to weather the storm of the accurate Tunney punches he would face in a return match.

"You'll have to fight Sharkey first," he said.

Dempsey could see the promoter's side of it. "I'll fight him anywhere and any time you say, Tex," he declared.

The place chosen was Yankee Stadium and the date was July 21, 1927. But the time was not a good one. Three days before the fight, Jack's favorite brother Johnny and his wife died in a terrible tragedy.

With this weighing on his mind, Jack was listless and depressed as he climbed through the ropes to meet the ambitious young man from Boston.

For five rounds Sharkey hit Jack as often and as hard as he wished. He danced around like a fast middleweight, throwing punches from every angle. Dempsey took the blows, fighting back sluggishly. It was clear to the crowd, most of whom were rooting for him to win, that he just didn't have it anymore.

Working over him frantically in his corner, Leo Flynn, tried to jar him out of his lethargy. "You're losing bad, Jack," he said tensely. "You'll never get a chance for the title."

Something in Dempsey — the same stubborn drive that had led him to win over heavy odds from the time of his youth — made him ignore his fatigue and determine to tear apart his opponent. He was not fighting as a champion should. He was not giving the fans what they had paid to see.

"Hit him in the body," Flynn shouted as the bell rang and Dempsey sprang from his corner.

Dempsey followed Flynn's advice, hurling his short but powerful hooks and uppercuts from a bobbing crouch and making Sharkey back away. The punishment continued throughout the round. In the seventh, trying to protect himself, Sharkey dropped his guard. That was enough for the Mauler. He slammed home a left to Sharkey's jaw and the ex-sailor crumpled to the canvas.

Tex Rickard cheered the loudest when the fight was over, and made immediate plans to contact Tunney. Because Gene was playing a vaudeville date in St. Louis, Tex chartered a special train to go there with the contract for the fight. Confident as usual and assured of a vast sum of money, Gene signed readily.

The fans were confident, too — that Jack was the killer of old. There were 104,000 of them crammed into Soldier's Field, Chicago, on September 22, 1927. The gate was an incredible $2,658,000. Tunney was to receive $990,000 — the largest amount any fighter had ever received. Dempsey's $450,000 was the largest sum a challenger had ever gotten.

The return match attracted more millionaires and celebrities from every field than any sporting event before or since.

To a newspaperman at ringside, Tex shouted exultantly, "Kid, if a thunderbolt struck the first ten rows, the world would stop. Because I've got there all the world's money, all the world's big shots, all the world's brains and all the world's talent."

Dempsey was greeted with a tremendous roar and he grinned happily as he clasped his gloves over his head in the boxer's salute. Thanks to his mountain training and the Sharkey fight, he was in top shape. But it was clear that the handsome Tunney had not let his own condition slide. He wore a cool expression and appeared not to notice that most of the fans were rooting for the ex-champion.

A former bantamweight titleholder, Dave Barry, was the referee. Calling both contestants to the center of the ring, he went over the "neutral-corner" rule. This was an Illinois

State Boxing Commission rule that, in the event of a knockdown, the fallen boxer's opponent must move to the farthest corner from him. Only when he had reached the corner would the referee start the count. The purpose of the rule was to keep the fallen boxer's opponent from standing over him and knocking him down again as he tried to get to his feet. Obviously, in many cases the fallen fighter would be defenseless and off balance as he rose. This rule was to cause the greatest argument in boxing history.

For six rounds, this fight followed the pattern of the first one. Dempsey would try to get close to Tunney to land one of his savage hooks. Tunney, cautious as usual, would slow down Dempsey with his accurate straight left and back away. Dempsey continued to press forward despite the blows that rained on his face, but it appeared he was tiring. Indeed, in the fourth round, Tunney fans rose to their feet, imploring Gene to knock out the groggy challenger. Jack took everything Tunney threw at him, however, and weathered the round. The minute's rest worked wonders for him, and in the fifth he was back in pursuit of Tunney.

In the seventh, spectators were furnished with a thrill that brought them up screaming. One third of the way through the round, Dempsey charged with his old ferocity, and in an exchange near the ropes, lashed a desperate long left to Tunney's jaw. As Tunney lost his balance and started to go down, Dempsey hit him with seven more frantic blows. Tunney was on the canvas! He fell in a sitting posture, eyes glazed, one glove resting on a ring rope. Clearly helpless, he wore a bewildered look.

The timekeeper began the count — *but referee Barry did not start counting.* Instead, he waved at Dempsey to go to the farthest corner. Many seconds went by before Jack — eager to pounce on Tunney again — moved to the corner

Barry designated. When Barry returned to the downed champion, he finally began the count. But by this time Gene had had about seven seconds to regain his senses. He retained enough wits to take the full nine count before rising, and by then — so good was his condition — he was again the alert, cautious Tunney.

In his training, Gene had practiced running backward. This stood him in good stead as he avoided any contact with Jack for the rest of the round. At one point, Jack was so disgusted with his inability to catch up to Gene that he stopped in center ring and asked Gene to stop running and fight. But Tunney was far too smart a ring general to do Dempsey's bidding.

The eighth round saw Gene completely recovered. Once again, he countered Dempsey's aggressiveness with stabbing lefts. In the ninth he actually sent Dempsey down for a short count. By now, Dempsey's face was raw from Tunney's blows. His eyebrows were cut, his lips were bleeding, and his mouth was puffed up.

Seeming to grow stronger as the fight progressed, Gene took complete command in the tenth. He kept jabbing and staggered Dempsey with right-hand blows to the heart, followed by straight lefts that made Jack's head rock back. At the final bell, Jack was exhausted, nearly out on his feet but still trying to land a haymaker.

It was clear that Tunney was the victor and his hand was raised by the referee. Immediately after the inevitable decision was made, an argument started among boxing fans — whether they had seen the fight or not — that continues to this day.

Dempsey supporters claim that Barry should have picked up the timekeeper's count at about six. If he had done so, Tunney would undoubtedly have been counted out. Tunney supporters say that Barry was right in not starting his count until Jack had moved to a neutral corner — and even so, Tunney could have gotten up earlier if he had been forced to. In any event, *The New York Times* gave the fight its biggest front-page headline:

GENE TUNNEY KEEPS TITLE BY DECISION AFTER
TEN ROUNDS; DEMPSEY INSISTS FOE WAS OUT IN
THE 7TH AND WILL APPEAL; 150,000 SEE CHICAGO
FIGHT, MILLIONS LISTEN ON RADIO

Influential sports figures who thought that Barry should have started his count at four or five instead of at one protested to the Illinois State Athletic Commission. They argued that Tunney should have been counted out in what has come to be known as "the fight of the long count." But the officials would not allow the protest. They claimed that if Dempsey (against his instincts) had backed off to a far corner, Barry would have picked up the timekeeper's count. But Jack had not. And therefore Barry was justified. It was one of the most controversial decisions in sports history. To this day thousands of fans believe that "Jack was robbed."

A third fight might have settled the issue, and Tunney graciously offered Dempsey a second return, but Jack refused. Estelle did not want to see him take any more battering, and Jack had no relish for the hard training he must do, at the age of thirty-three, to stand up to a punishing marksman like Tunney. But the main reason for Jack's unwillingness to fight Gene was the death of Tex Rickard.

Tex had made Jack his partner in promotion — something of which Jack was very proud. Jack helped him promote a fight between Tunney and Australian Tom Heeney in June, 1928. But with Dempsey at a desk instead of in the ring, the fight did not draw well and the promotion lost money. After easily defeating Heeney, Tunney retired as heavyweight champion. The title was put up for grabs, to be finally won by Max Schmeling of Germany, who beat Jack Sharkey on a foul.

But Rickard did not see this development. Three months after he and Dempsey went into partnership, he was attacked by appendicitis. Jack, in Detroit at the time, flew to Miami to be at Rickard's bedside. Tex died in his arms and Dempsey wept unashamedly.

Years later, in dedicating a stadium to Rickard, Jack said, "All the glory, all the wealth I ever won, I owe to Tex Rickard. He was like a father to me."

Business had to go on, and Jack took over the promotion of the fight between Billy "Kid" Stribling and Jack Sharkey in Miami on June 6, 1929. This was Jack's farewell to boxing in the Twenties, after eight years of being its most colorful figure and for most of that time unquestionably its greatest fighter. Officially, Jack's record immediately following the second Tunney bout was 65 fights, of which he won 47 by knockout, 7 by decision and one by a foul. He had 5 no-decision fights, lost 4 decisions and was knocked out once.

But the record will also show that Jack, the wild and terrifying ringman of that wild and noisy decade, symbolized much that was held in high regard by a growing, optimistic, carefree America. He rose from poverty to riches, from loneliness to fame and from eating stew with hobos to dining with princes. And he did it by adhering to a philosophy he picked up as a hungry young drifter: "I've got to smash him before he smashes me." It found great appeal in an era of thumping jazz music, bootleggers, speakeasies, perilous adventures in the air, a loosening of moral codes and a prosperity that seemed endless. The exciting killer of the ring who was Dempsey suited its mood exactly.

A man of Dempsey's stature and likeable qualities was bound to become involved in a flurry of projects. In the Thirties, he got into politics as a supporter of Herbert H. Lehman and Franklin D. Roosevelt, launched a candy bar, refereed professional wrestling matches, produced a pair of motion pictures, started restaurants and invested in oil wells. In the heart of the Depression, he even returned to the ring, knocking over about 175 Humpty Dumpties. He was urged, as a matter of fact, to consider fighting Sharkey (who had taken the title from Max Schmeling in a return bout) for the championship. But Jack got a severe lacing from Kingfish Levinsky — himself an old-timer as boxers go — and abandoned thoughts of a comeback.

When war broke out, Jack tried to enlist in the Army. This branch of the armed forces said he was too old, but the Coast Guard accepted him. Like Tunney in the Navy, he was commissioned and was put in charge of getting recruits into shape. Later he took part in the invasion of Okinawa, even capturing a fleeing Japanese soldier. For his services to his country, he was awarded the Legion of Merit.

Jack now spends most of his time as proprietor of Jack Dempsey's Restaurant in New York City, though he still maintains a strong interest in boxing. A few times he has sponsored or managed promising fighters, none of whom have ever gotten very far. Perhaps they were not hungry enough.

BILLY MITCHELL
Air Force Leader

Billy Mitchell always said what he meant. He wasn't a patient man and he wasn't a tactful one. He had a knack of seeing things clearly, things that other men could not or would not see. When he came to a decision, he wasn't the type of man to keep it to himself. He let the world know about it.

Years before World War I began, Billy Mitchell came back from Alaska with the certain knowledge that the United States was in store for trouble from the East.

"Sooner or later we will be at war with Japan," he said then. "We want the China trade, and so do they, and there's going to be more and more friction between us. Sooner or later there will be a war."

He would repeat this theory many times over the years. But no one listened to him. In 1941, Japanese planes took the American Fleet completely by surprise at Pearl Harbor, striking an almost fatal blow at American naval strength. Billy Mitchell's prophecy had come true. America had ignored his words, and the results were disastrous.

The prospects of a war with Japan were not the only theory that Billy Mitchell kept spouting. Throughout World War I, he had begun to develop an understanding of the tremendous importance of air power in modern warfare. Nowadays it seems obvious that air strength is absolutely vital for any military power, but when Mitchell first began to make his point, his ideas were revolutionary.

Everyone thought they knew what made the difference in a war. It was the Navy that won the battles: unsinkable battleships and sleek swift cruisers, flanked by maneuverable destroyers — ships like this would keep America safe and strong. Airplanes? Oh, they were interesting enough, and valuable for special jobs. They were handy for reconnaissance and communications. They were useful for scouting enemy positions and pinpointing targets for the artillery. But as far as the first line of offense went, airplanes were next to useless.

At least that was what everyone thought. Everyone but Billy Mitchell. He was a man with a vision, a man with a message for his nation. He could visualize a sort of warfare never seen on earth, warfare in which heavy bombers leveled industrial plants and sent battleships to the bottom of the ocean. His visions made him a great military prophet. They also got him into trouble.

Almost from the moment the Armistice was signed ending World War I, Billy Mitchell functioned as America's leading exponent of military aviation. He outlined his views loud and clear. He took publicity wherever he found it, writing articles, giving interviews, speaking his mind without regard for the consequences. He barnstormed the country, talking about the future of aviation to anyone who would listen.

Mitchell didn't mince words. As far as he was concerned, there was a lot to criticize about the way America's defenses were being managed. He was a military man, a Brigadier General, and he wasn't supposed to criticize his superiors in the War Department. This didn't stop him. He said what he wanted to say, and he said it so forcefully that it was impossible to ignore his words.

Some people listened. Some people supported the young general with the firm, clear voice. Others wanted to shut him up as quickly as possible.

When a military man goes against the wishes of his superiors — when he criticizes official policy and puts his case before the general public — the outcome is inevitable. Billy Mitchell was brought before a court-martial. The charges were deliberately vague. He was accused of actions and behavior unbecoming to an officer — charges which meant everything and nothing. On February 1, 1926, his sentence went into effect. His rank was reduced to private and he was stripped of pay for a five-year period. Under those conditions, Billy Mitchell had no alternatives; he submitted his resignation from the Army and returned to private life.

In a sense, this was his own fault. He could have gone along with his superior officers. He could have paid lip service to official government policy. He could have spoken tactfully, could have made his views known in a more polite fashion.

But he just wasn't that kind of a man.

William Mitchell was born in Nice, France, on December 29, 1879, the first son of a wealthy banker who later pioneered in scientific farming. Billy spent his boyhood in

Wisconsin, where he developed a firm love for the outdoors that would last him all his life. He learned to ride a horse and handle a rifle. He hunted, he fished. A natural leader, he was respected in and out of school.

By the time the Spanish-American war broke out, Billy was a student at Columbian College in Washington, D.C., where his family then lived. His father, John Lendrum Mitchell, was the respected Senator from Wisconsin, a leading supporter of world peace. But war with Spain seemed to be inevitable, and when the battleship *Maine* was blown up in Havana Harbor, the choice was clear. America had to go to war.

The day Congress voted for war, Billy made up his mind. He went to his father at once to inform him of his decision. "I'm joining the Army," he said. "I'm going to enlist."

"Why not finish school?" his father advised. "You could get a commission as an officer."

Billy shook his head. Even then he had learned to come to a decision quickly and to stand by it whatever the consequences. "I'll enlist as a private," he said. "I don't care about a commission."

He was eighteen years old and a private in the First Wisconsin Infantry, already impatient to see overseas combat duty in Cuba. But his natural aptitude for military life and his native leadership ability did not escape notice. He had never asked for a commission. One was granted to him anyway. He was a Second Lieutenant assigned to the Second Volunteer Signal Corps.

All Billy wanted was to get to Cuba, but this was a chance that never seemed to come. Spain began negotiating for peace before he received an overseas assignment. Finally, after the war was over, he got the chance to serve in the

190

Army of Occupation in Cuba. He grabbed the chance and made the most of it.

The next year, another war was in progress. According to the treaty signed with Spain, the United States had taken control of a number of Spanish possessions, including the Philippine Islands. Guerrillas in the Philippines, under the leadership of Emilio Aguinaldo, began an armed insurrection. Mitchell was anxious for a taste of combat. When it looked as though he would not be sent to the Philippines, he began pulling strings, even attempting to resign his commission and enlist all over again as a private. Instead, he was made a First Lieutenant and sent overseas, where he distinguished himself by developing a superb network of telegraph communications for the American forces. He became Acting Chief Signal Officer and helped set up the eventual capture of the wily rebel chieftain.

By the time he returned to the United States, Billy Mitchell had come to an important decision. He was going to make the military service his career. This was a big decision. He was a rich man's son, and he could easily have settled down in civilian life, managing a bank or a farm or devoting himself to politics. It was rare for a wealthy young man to choose Army life in those days. Billy had found his place, though, and he stuck to his decision.

In 1901, he went to Alaska. Ever since the Territory had been purchased from Russia in 1867, the American Government had not known what to do with it. Cold and vast, the Alaskan wilderness had seemed useless at first. Then, after the Klondike gold strike, Americans had begun to realize its true value.

Now the chief problem was one of communication. Marconi's wireless had not yet come into being, and telegraph wires were necessary to get news from one place to another.

Billy took the job of getting a telegraphy system set up in the frozen Territory. Men who knew Alaska couldn't believe he had a chance to put his methods into effect, but Billy stuck to his guns and worked himself and his men hard. His superiors in Washington had hoped he could do the job in four years. Mitchell himself predicted that he would manage it in half that time, and he wound up beating his own rigorous schedule by a wide margin. By the time he returned to the United States, he had been rewarded with a captaincy. It was obvious that here was a young officer with a future.

It was about this time that Billy Mitchell began to get interested in aviation. Aeronautics was not even an infant science by then. A few experiments had been made, a handful of books published, but the Wright Brothers had not yet taken off on their historic flight at Kitty Hawk when Billy Mitchell first began to study every book he could get his hands on that dealt with aviation.

Perhaps he realized that this new field would be his most important interest in life. But at the time it was only a sideline. He went on advancing in his profession, handling every assignment that came his way and making a name for himself.

He was already becoming widely known as an outspoken man. Even as the youngest officer on the General Staff at Washington, he was becoming noted for his willingness to sound off and speak his mind.

In 1914, war broke out in Europe. World War I had been building up a head of steam, and a minor incident — the assassination of an Austrian archduke by a Serbian fanatic — touched off the inevitable outbreak of hostilities. From the outset, some of the more perceptive men in America realized that we would be drawn into the war before it was

192

over. Billy Mitchell was among them. Long before the United States entered the war, he was busy making plans to ensure American preparedness.

At the time, not even Billy Mitchell had a clear idea of the ultimate importance of that new invention, the airplane. Like so many other men, he thought of it as a limited device at best, useful for reconnaissance and valuable to a branch of the Army such as the Signal Corps. But as time went by, Mitchell, now assigned to the Aviation Service, began to realize that the airplane was destined to play a far more important role in military tactics. So certain was he of the importance of the airplane, and so interested was he in aviation, that he was determined to learn all there was to know about flying.

He had to gain this knowledge on his own. He was thirty-six years old and had been promoted to the rank of major, and the Army was unwilling to train a man of his age and rank as a pilot. Mitchell went ahead on his own, using his own money to put himself through flying school. He gave up his free time to take lessons, working long and hard to master the complicated techniques that it took to manage the flying crates that were the airplanes of the time.

In 1917, America entered the war. It had become impossible to remain neutral any longer. Almost at once Billy Mitchell was sent to France to familiarize himself with the situation there and to make firsthand acquaintance with wartime aviation. It was his duty to make American air forces equal to the task ahead of them, and he meant to do his job well.

Anyone familiar with modern air combat would have a hard time understanding the use of the airplane in World War I. While the planes themselves were often poorly engineered and unreliable, the uses to which they were put were considerably less ambitious in the light of modern advances. Reconnaissance was the airplane's chief function. Planes would soar out over a battlefield, and pilots would set their awkward crates down on their landing strips and report on what they had seen. The use of an airplane for offense was truly primitive.

At the beginning of the war, pilots would carry handguns with them in the cockpits of their planes. They would use these guns to fire out at other pilots in other planes. Gradually this system was refined. At first, pilots began to carry machine guns; later, guns were built into the planes themselves.

But the tremendous potential of the airplane was never realized. The use of planes to strafe infantry positions, to bomb supply depots, to attack troop trains — all of these possibilities never seemed to occur to the men who ran the war. To be sure, many of the planes themselves were not up to par for this sort of activity, but they were capable of a great deal more than the role cut out for them.

Colonel Billy Mitchell — he had been promoted — was quick to realize this. As head of the Air Service, he constantly campaigned for more planes and more men to fly them. He already saw two things — that American air forces were woefully behind the forces of the Allies and the Germans alike, and that air power would be the key to the future. Whatever use was made of the airplane in World War I, it would hold the balance of power between nations in any wars that might follow.

Perhaps this should have been obvious to everyone. It certainly seems obvious enough now. When Mitchell's fliers began to launch bombing runs on the enemy, men of imagination should have been able to realize the tremendous improvements which might be made in planes and in bombs as well, and the destructive power which aerial weapons would furnish.

In any event, the daring young colonel had found a field of interest that would grip him for the rest of his life. He had been interested in aviation before and had retained more than a passing interest in it ever since his tour of duty in Alaska. Now it became his chief passion. Throughout the war he devoted himself completely to the task of developing and refining American air power. When the war ended in victory, he came home with only one objective in mind. He wanted to develop the American Air Service to meet the challenges of the twentieth century.

Billy Mitchell was a month shy of thirty-nine years old when the Armistice was signed on November 11, 1918. He was a hero famous throughout the country and the world. Air warfare in Europe, however insignificant, had caught the fancy of the public. The fighter pilots were the darlings of the age, and Billy Mitchell, now Brigadier General, came home covered with decorations and medals.

The war was over. In the minds of Americans everywhere, it was not only the first world war but the last one as well. It had been fought to make the world safe for democracy. National leaders and average citizens all looked forward to a time when war would cease forever and men would live in peace and harmony. The terrors of the war had been beyond anything in history; the prospect of another war was unthinkable.

Mitchell knew better. Even as one war ended, he could see the prospects of another looming in the future. The German military machine had not been dismantled, and German dreams of glory lay sleeping, only waiting for a leader to come along and revive them once again. The specter of

Japanese hopes for expansion hovered in the East. Billy Mitchell had recognized the possibilities of war with Japan long ago; now his convictions grew stronger. He was determined that America have a strong air force. Planes had to be built and men had to be trained to fly them if America was going to stay at the helm of world power.

The America Billy Mitchell came home to did not want to hear about future wars or the need for a strong air force. Americans were glad that the war was over; they wanted to take it easy now — give themselves up completely to a world of flappers and bathtub gin, a world of strident jazz music and all of the madcap pleasures that were the mark of the Twenties.

Military leaders, on the other hand, did not want anything to disturb the current state of affairs. They had their own ideas of how an army should be maintained, ideas reinforced with the experience of generations. They knew that a country needed two things to win wars — strength at sea and strength on the ground. And they did not want an upstart one-star general with a closet full of medals telling them how to run things.

A more methodical, less boisterous, man might have done his work quietly and cautiously. That was not Billy Mitchell's style. He saw his duty clearly and he couldn't understand why the rest of the country didn't see things his way. He wanted appropriations for more planes. The Navy wanted money to build bigger and better ships. The way Mitchell saw things, this made the Naval leaders his enemies. If he was going to improve the Air Force, it would have to be at the expense of the Navy.

He fell to work with a vengeance. He criticized the Navy openly, stumping the country to argue that the Navy was a throwback to another time, that battleships and cruisers

196

would be useless when another war was fought. Ships were sitting ducks, he argued. A plane could swoop down from the skies and send any boat in the ocean to the bottom. Take the money away from the Navy, he urged, and spend that money to build the most powerful air force in the world.

There were men who believed in him — men who had the imagination to see what Billy Mitchell was talking about. But there were plenty of others who thought the young general out of his mind. After all, they pointed out, it had been the Navy that had won the war. The naval blockade of Germany had turned the tide while Billy Mitchell's airmen were making a big show of shooting other planes out of the skies. It seemed painfully obvious to them that a strong Navy was the key to a strong defense.

If General Mitchell had simply asked for money for the Air Service, he would not have made so many powerful enemies. His requests might have been denied, but no one would have resented his campaign. But a man asking for appropriations was one thing, and a man who went around demanding that the Navy's budget be reduced was something else entirely. In no time at all, Billy Mitchell had managed to start a one-man war with the Navy Department. All of its top officers were after his scalp.

Meanwhile, it began to look as though the government couldn't care less about aviation. The Air Service was placed under the official command of a ground-forces leader with no aviation experience. Airplanes were no longer being built, and men failed to see their possible importance either in war or peace.

Billy Mitchell could see the future. He predicted that airmail would one day become standard, that letters would be speeded on their way aboard huge modern transport planes. He visualized a commercial air service that would

carry passengers across the country in a fraction of the time
it took them by train. A few people listened to him and
shared his dream, but most shook their heads and told themselves that Mitchell was out of his mind.

His war with the Navy grew louder and more bitter. He
began to take his case to the public — a habit that would get
him into trouble before long. He wrote magazine articles
and gave out newspaper interviews by the score. Soon his
case boiled down to one powerful argument — that airplanes equipped with high-power bombs could sink any
ship afloat.

He was to have a chance to prove his boast. The Navy
held several German ships which had been captured during
the war. According to the terms of the Armistice, these ships
had to be destroyed. The Navy planned to sink them by
blowing holes in their sides from the guns of their largest
battleship. Mitchell demanded the chance to prove his point.

"The ships are going to be sunk anyway," he said. "Let
me show you what airplanes can do."

Negotiations proceeded slowly. Finally the Navy accepted
the challenge. Mitchell and his ace pilots would have an
opportunity, once and for all, to pit their planes and bombs
against German ships.

In the summer of 1921, the contest finally got under way.
Fliers from all over the country assembled under Billy
Mitchell's guidance to give the Navy and the nation a lesson
in the power of the airplane. Four captured German vessels
floated in the Atlantic, waiting for Mitchell to show his stuff.

Two of the ships were easy prey. A German U-boat with
tin armor and a light destroyer did not pose much of a challenge to his air power. But the two larger German ships were
not such a simple matter. A cruiser, heavily armored, posed

a challenge, and the German battleship *Ostfriesland* was a formidable target. It seemed impossible for Mitchell's men to sink such a powerful vessel.

Billy Mitchell was sure of himself and of his men. Ever ready to pick up publicity and get in a subtle dig at the Navy, he let newsreel photographers take pictures of a pile of bombs with REGARDS TO THE NAVY painted on them. This was a brilliant publicity device, but it won him plenty of enemies. One important official actually petitioned the Secretary of War to have Mitchell removed from office. The petition was denied, but Mitchell's opponents were banded together more tightly.

While the nation waited, the tests began. The little U-boat was the first target, and the Navy sent out planes of its own to sink the submarine. A series of lightweight bombs from Naval planes quickly sank it. If nothing else, this seemed to prove that an airplane could hit a small target. But the major tests lay ahead.

The destroyer came next. Again the target was a light ship and no great challenge, but this time it was Mitchell's turn and his men put on a good show. First, fighter pilots strafed the ship's deck in a display of firing power; then bombers soared in and plastered the ship from bow to stern. It took only twenty minutes from the time the first bomb landed on the deck of the German destroyer until the ship was on its way to the ocean bottom.

For the cruiser, the 5,000-ton *Frankfurt*, Mitchell brought out a surprise. He had managed to figure out that the best way to sink a ship was not with a direct hit but with a near miss. If a bomb came close to the target and exploded full force in the water beside the vessel, the water served to magnify the power of the blast tremendously. After a few direct hits on the powerful *Frankfurt*, one of Mitchell's men scored a near miss that landed in the water after glancing off the forecastle deck. The mighty cruiser was finished by that one explosion. She rocked back, tipped forward, and began to go down. Two more direct hits only added insult to injury. The *Frankfurt* sank to the bottom.

Even after this dazzling exhibition, few men seriously believed that Mitchell had a chance to sink the *Ostfriesland*. Mitchell's men were anxious to prove their strength, and the cocky general himself was busy organizing the plan of attack. At first the bombs did not seem to be doing much damage, but what observers did not realize was that Billy Mitchell's near misses were softening the hull of the giant ship. Time after time the planes winged out and sent their deadly cargo spinning downward at the German ship; bomb after bomb struck home and did its damage. Finally, to the surprise of all onlookers and to the utter dismay of the Navy, the battleship pitched and rolled and took on more and more water until she gave up the fight and went down.

Billy Mitchell had proved his point in the most dramatic fashion possible. No one could question the value of air power now. Never again could a battleship be regarded as unsinkable. His planes had scored a great victory — one that echoed across the nation and around the world.

Mitchell had scored amazingly. Now was the time for him to turn diplomat, time for him to push his advantage tactfully. Tact, however, was still something he had never managed to develop. Patience was also an unknown Mitchell quality. If he had rested on his laurels — if he had devoted himself quietly and calmly to building the air force that was his dream — his story might have ended on a different note.

Instead, he stormed ahead in his usual way. He was a hero with the public, and he pushed this advantage, making speeches that were loud and fiery, giving interviews that said just what he wanted to say. In a nation where everyone was busy enjoying the pleasures of peace, Billy Mitchell was almost alone in foreseeing the horrors of war. He never lost his conviction that war was coming, and he was tortured by fears that his America would be unprepared for war when it finally did come.

The country, carefree and prosperous, did not want to give Mitchell the money he needed to build the kind of air force he wanted. They wouldn't agree to his demands, and he in turn would not soften his requests. Time after time, he threatened to resign when his recommendations were denied; time after time, he stayed, giving himself up completely to the job at hand.

He was no longer as young as he had been. Years of hard living had taken their toll, and his heart was not as sound as it might have been. But he never slowed his pace. He had never learned to take it easy, and he wasn't starting now — not with such a huge job ahead of him. Even his free time was given over to hard pursuits. He hunted, fished, hiked — and then he threw himself back into the task of building an air force.

The last straw came soon enough. A Navy dirigible, the *Shenandoah*, embarked on a goodwill flight in bad weather. In a violent electrical storm, the blimp and all men aboard it were lost. This needless tragedy infuriated Mitchell — it seemed a complete waste to him, a horrible disaster that should never have happened.

He would not be muzzled. Instead of letting officials hush up the tragedy, he insisted on criticizing the men in charge in unmistakable terms. The outcome was inevitable. Billy Mitchell was brought before a court-martial, charged with actions and behavior unbecoming to an officer. He was found guilty, despite the arguments of many flying men that everything he had said had been absolutely correct. He was stripped of his rank and his pay, forced to resign, and left to find his own way in a country that had decided it was better off without his services.

Even then, Billy Mitchell refused to let himself be put out to pasture. A private citizen now, he could say whatever he wanted to say without worrying about official interference. Two themes ran through all that he said or wrote: on the one hand, he stressed the utter necessity of a strong and independent air force, completely free of external domination; and on the other, he continued to point out the ever-increasing danger of war with Japan.

He never let up on either point. Doctors told him to rest, explaining that his heart could not stand the pace forever. Billy Mitchell would not listen to them. He went on a coast-to-coast lecture tour. He ground out article after article, gave countless interviews, kept up an unceasing correspondence with people all over the country.

When the Japanese invaded Manchuria in 1931, Mitchell's was one of the few voices raised against them. Many people saw the war as a matter that concerned only Japan and China. Mitchell saw it differently. He realized that this was only the beginning in a huge plan of Japanese aggression. And in the years to follow, as both Japan and Germany built up their military strengths as rapidly as possible, he knew that he had been right. He predicted that Japan would attack by surprise, without going through the formality of war. On December 7, 1941, the Japanese Air Force dramatically proved his prophecy.

Billy Mitchell was not alive when the Japanese attacked Pearl Harbor. Years of overexertion had taken their toll long before that day. In February, 1936, at fifty-five years of age and exhausted by years of speaking and writing and working for his country, Billy Mitchell suffered a fatal heart attack.

The country tried to forget him. Japan was testing its military strength on China; Hitler was readying an army of conquest in Germany. But America went on living in peace and expecting that peace would last forever. Billy Mitchell's warnings went unheeded.

Eleven years after he died, his countrymen began to realize how very right he had been. The war he had predicted had taken place, and the air power he had so strongly supported had turned the tide of it. Never again would the importance of a strong air force be ignored. Now, with his predictions come true, a nation acknowledged its debt to the man it had pushed out of the limelight. He was given a posthumous promotion to the rank of Major General. After his death, Billy Mitchell, scorned during his lifetime, finally won the honors he deserved.

AMELIA EARHART
Queen of the Skies

The little girl from Kansas was celebrating her ninth birthday on a summer day in 1907. With her parents and sister Muriel, she had recently moved from Atchison, Kansas, to Des Moines, Iowa. Now her father was taking the two girls to the State Fair for a birthday celebration.

Amelia was having the time of her life. She had already had one pony ride and wanted another. She and Muriel had been on the merry-go-round until they were happily sick to their stomachs. They wore funny paper hats on their heads and begged their father for another pony ride.

But Edwin Earhart had something else in mind. There was an airplane at the fair, a plane similar to the one the Wright brothers had flown just four years before at Kitty Hawk. The plane was scheduled to give a demonstration ride, and Edwin Earhart was anxious to have a look at it.

Flight was man's oldest dream, an ancient myth and legend suddenly and unbelievably brought to reality. Few Americans understood what kept a plane in the air. Fewer still dared risk their lives in one of the primitive wood-and-metal crates. But thousands of Americans were excited about the possibilities of flight and impatient to see an actual demonstration. Edwin Earhart shared this excitement and interest.

His daughters did not. He had to drag them along to the edge of the flying field. Then, as the three of them stood among the crowd of watchers, young Amelia looked at the plane and wondered what the shouting was about. The aircraft looked unsound and ridiculous — a mass of wood and wire held together as much by hope as anything else — and she thought it would fall apart long before it got off the ground. It moved, picked up speed, suddenly left the ground and took off into the air. Amelia remained unimpressed. She could not have cared less.

No one who was with her that July day could have guessed what life had in store for her. The little Kansas tomboy would grow up to be the first lady of aviation, holding dozens of records, would be presented with the keys of countless cities and the medals of countless societies. She would be the first woman to cross the Atlantic in a plane; later, she would become the first woman to make the same trip in a solo flight. She would crash time and time again, scrambling from the wreckage of each airplane only to return to the skies once more. And at last there would come a day when she would try her final flight, a daring trip undertaken in the effort to become the first woman to fly around the world. She would crash and disappear forever, leaving a world to ponder her fate.

Amelia Earhart was never an ordinary sort of person. She was born July 24, 1898, in Atchison. Her father was a claims agent for the railroad, away a great deal of the time, and Amelia spent most of her childhood with her grandparents. She was an out-and-out tomboy, always busy, always on the move. She searched caves for Indian relics, flew a sled off the barn roof on an improvised roller coaster, played baseball and basketball and football like a boy.

She had a quick and original mind. She spent hours reading, her attention quickly absorbed by one subject after another. She was inventive, impatient, stubborn. Her parents were people who believed that a child should find his own way of growing — people who felt that all new experiences were educational. They encouraged Amelia's independence and she profited from it.

In 1917, Amelia took a trip to Toronto with her mother. There her independence showed itself, along with her concern for other people. At that time, the Canadians had been at war for over three years but America had not entered the conflict. On the streets of Toronto, Amelia saw wounded soldiers swathed in bandages, their faces drawn. She made up her mind at once, told her mother and made her decision stick — she would stay in Toronto to nurse the wounded.

Amelia remained in Toronto until the war's end, working as a nurse's aide. And it was there that her love of airplanes first came to the surface. Many of the wounded men she helped were fliers, and there was an airfield not far from the hospital. She would go to the field, watch planes taking off and landing, and watch aerial maneuvers. Time and time again, she begged to be taken up in a plane, but left Toronto without ever getting her wish. She didn't know it, but by this time the pattern of her life had been established.

At the war's end, Amelia went to New York. In 1919, she enrolled at Columbia University as a premedical student. She took a heavy study load, and worked hard and well. A year later she was in California, once more with her family.

Again, she and her father went to watch airplanes, but this time it was Amelia who did the coaxing. At an air meet at Daugherty Field, they saw planes like those they had seen in Toronto, but to Amelia's eyes there was a difference. The planes in Canada had been flown only by military aviators; no civilians could even have hoped to ride in them, much less fly them. These planes, though, were for civilian use.

Amelia thrilled with excitement. From an official at the field, she learned that the cost of flying lessons was around $1,000.

She knew at once what she had to do. Somehow or other, she must learn to fly; one way or another, she had to get her hands on $1,000 and learn to pilot a plane. First, she persuaded her father to let her go up in a plane as a passenger. A pilot took her up to 2,000 feet, but the ride ended too quickly to satisfy the slender young woman from Atchison. She left the cockpit of the little plane even more determined to learn to fly on her own.

A thousand dollars! It was more than Edwin Earhart could afford, but this did not stop Amelia. She found work at the telephone company in Los Angeles, and saved her money for flying lessons.

A woman named Neta Snook was her first instructor. They went up together every weekend, and bit by bit, Amelia began to master the difficult art of aviation. It did not come easy to her. Other would-be pilots took lesson after lesson, often getting their wings in a week or so through constant practice. Amelia had only weekends. She took her lessons when she could, learning slowly but well.

She was halfway through her lessons when Neta Snook suddenly quit as her teacher — the woman flier had been forced to sell her plane. Amelia found a man to teach her. She insisted that he instruct her in some elements of stunt flying as well, so that she would have a thorough grounding in all the elements of flight before she soloed. She did rolls and loops, Immelmann turns and dives and slips, getting everything down pat until she and her instructor both knew that she was ready.

Her first flight — a takeoff held back until a collapsed shock absorber had been replaced, then a climb skyward, a series of loops and rolls, finally the descent and a less than perfect landing. But as she walked away from her plane Amelia Earhart felt more than the surge of pride that follows the mastery of a difficult subject. She had found her place in life and in the world. The sensation of flying, the thrill of it, the joy of being master of one's fate with an airplane to operate as an extension of one's own body . . .

This was excitement, and triumph. And it was for her.

Amelia's enthusiasm never diminished. She took to the air like a bird, and nothing could take the thrill out of it for her. There were dangerous moments: one plane upended during an emergency landing and left her hanging upside-down in the cockpit; another flipped over even more violently and sent her soaring out of the cockpit. The danger never scared her enough to make her give up flying; the danger was simply part of the game.

By 1922, she owned her own plane, a Kinner Canary. But simple flying was not enough to satisfy Amelia. Aviation was a very new field, and she was one of its pioneers. She wanted not only to fly, but to fly as others had not yet flown. She wanted to set records — of distance, altitude, speed.

She set her first record in the little yellow Canary. She was trying for an altitude record, and she took the small plane to 14,000 feet — higher than anyone had flown a

Canary before then. It was no mean accomplishment for anyone, least of all for a woman, but the records she would set in years to come would make this one almost insignificant.

The Twenties were very special years for women. They had the right to vote, a privilege just recently granted. They were holding jobs in greater numbers than ever before, and the jobs they held were of greater importance than those previously entrusted to women. The career woman was beginning to make her presence known in American life. Women who did things, women who made a deep impression upon their country, drew tremendous notice and frequently became celebrities overnight.

In the same way, flying was drawing great attention from the American public. Every year brought fresh proof of man's triumph over the law of gravity. Better and better planes were designed, and better and better men began to fly them. The idea of a man alone in the heavens, flying alone with the stars for guidance and the odds sometimes stacked heavily against him, caught the imagination of the nation.

Perhaps the most exciting event in aviation took place in 1927, when Lindbergh made his historic nonstop flight from New York to Paris — a flight that had the whole world hailing him as a hero.

If you put together both of these elements — a woman and an airplane — then you had an event that would truly make newspaper headlines. In 1928, a woman flier, Mrs. Frederick Guest, decided to perfect just such a combination. She bought a plane, planning to fly it from New York to London. But Mrs. Guest had a husband and children, and the risk of a transatlantic flight was more than she felt she could take. Still, she did not give up the project entirely.

She herself would not go — but some other young aviatrix could go in her place, as a passenger if not as a pilot. All she had to do was find a woman to make the trip.

A number of people helped Mrs. Guest arrange the flight. They scouted around to find out who the best female fliers were, drawing up lists of prospects and checking them out carefully. In time, their choice narrowed down to one woman.

Her name was Amelia Earhart.

She was in Boston by then, working at a settlement house as a social worker. She had done a great deal of flying since she had first bought the Kinner Canary, but she had never attempted to make a career out of aviation. She went on flying while she began to make a place for herself in social work. An attractive and modern young woman, as well as an expert flier, a woman doing interesting and socially beneficial work — all of these factors made her all the more potent a symbol of America's emerging young women, and all the more desirable as a passenger on the flight across the ocean.

Amelia accepted the proposal at once. Lindbergh's flight had fired her imagination just as it had thrilled the world. The flight would certainly be dangerous, and Amelia did not brush aside the dangers. She even wrote letters to her parents, letters to be mailed in the event that the flight was a failure that cost her life.

"Hooray for the last grand adventure," she wrote her father. "I wish I had won, but it was worthwhile anyway." And she echoed these sentiments to her mother, assuring her that "Even though I have lost, the adventure was worthwhile."

Gradually the preparations were made. The plane was the *Friendship*, a trimotor Fokker which Mrs. Guest had

purchased from Admiral Byrd. Wilmer L. Stultz was selected as pilot, Slim Gordon as mechanic. The details of the
flight were set. The *Friendship* would leave from Boston,
proceed to Trepassey, Newfoundland, and then make the
flight from Trepassey to England. The men worked on the
plane, modifying its design, replacing the front wheels with
pontoons, and doing everything they could to ensure a successful trip.

Time after time the takeoff from Boston was postponed
because of weather conditions. Finally the *Friendship* took
off, made an unscheduled landing in Halifax, and completed the jump to Trepassey.

For fifteen days the *Friendship* remained on the ground
at Trepassey, held there by strong winds and dismally bad
weather. Time and time again, Bill Stultz tried to get the
plane into the air, each time without success. The weather
damaged the little plane, causing an oil tank to crack and a
pontoon to spring a leak. Slim Gordon repaired the plane
each time, and the crew of three waited for good weather.

Waiting was hard for Amelia Earhart. If the prospect of
a flight across the ocean was hazardous to begin with, the
endless waiting in the frozen town of Trepassey could
hardly have made things easier for her. But she waited as
patiently as she could.

Finally, on June 17th, the weather improved slightly. It
took three takeoff attempts before Bill Stultz got the plane
airborne. At last he was successful. The little plane climbed
through banks of fog, hit a sudden snowstorm. Harsh winds
knocked it about roughly. Updrafts would bounce the plane
higher; downdrafts would pull the *Friendship*'s nose down
again. The three-motored Fokker flew onward, maintaining
a steady speed slightly over a hundred miles an hour.

The weather cleared all at once. The sky was blue, a clear

and brilliant blue. Below, the ocean was beautifully calm.
The ocean! Amelia stared down at it. They were doing it,
she told herself. They were flying across the Atlantic Ocean,
and she was the first woman in history to make the trip.

It was not a bad flight, once the first skirmish with foul
weather was over. It was well timed — Stultz sighted land
just as the gas tanks were beginning to run dangerously
low. The *Friendship* had held course well, and Stultz
smoothly touched down on the water offshore of Burry Port
in Wales. They had done it — they had crossed the ocean
and they were safe.

Amelia was excited at first, but worn out from the flight,
from the tension, from the glory. Soon the excitement wore
off. She was the first woman to cross the Atlantic, she
thought — but so what? She had done almost nothing.
Stultz had flown all the way while she lay on the floor taking
pictures and filling up space. After all, she told herself, she
had been nothing more than baggage on the *Friendship*.

Someday, she thought, maybe she would try it alone.

What a reception she got! Amelia might shrug off her feat
as nothing very important, but the rest of the world was not
prepared to dismiss it so briefly. The two weeks she spent in
England were a constant round of teas and parties and din-
ners, of interviews by the score. She was a celebrity, whether
she felt herself worthy of the honor or not.

The reception was even greater when she returned to
America. She made a perfect symbol, an ideal hero for
Americans in 1928. A courageous young woman, a flier, a
combination of the new spirit of womanhood with the new
frontier of aviation. Cities vied to claim her as a native
daughter or to present her with their keys. She was mobbed
by autograph hounds, besieged with invitations to speak to

213

organizations, to give interviews, to write articles for publication.

G. P. Putnam, one of the men who had led in planning the flight, helped Amelia write her memoirs of the flight and aided her in her business decisions. Within a few months, she had received over $50,000 for her efforts — a sum far greater than she had ever expected. And all she had done was to lie on the floor of the plane like a sack of flour!

This bothered her more and more. She could not help feeling that she was accepting money and fame under false pretenses, that she was being hailed as something she was not. The world considered her a great flier, but the only flying she had done had been relatively routine flights at home, nothing to compare with a transatlantic trip. At first she felt guilty.

Then her feelings of guilt changed to determination. She had received great praise as a flier — she would just have to go ahead and become one. She had won fame for doing next to nothing; now she was firm in her resolve to do something worthy of that fame. If the world insisted on making a celebrity out of her, she would live up to it.

She had the time now, and the money. She bought a plane, a small Aero Avian, and practiced with it relentlessly. She took off on a solo flight across America — a flight marked by several crashes and emergency landings, from each of which she emerged miraculously unhurt. On more than one occasion she had to wait while her plane was being repaired. Then she was airborne again, off on another leg of her cross-country flight. She made the trip successfully in spite of all the accidents and near crashes, and when it was over she felt she had gained back a certain measure of her self-respect. She was flying now, and not just making little local hops at that; she was proving herself in the air.

At the same time she felt a strong responsibility to the whole field of aviation. The urge to publicize flying had been one of her strongest motives in going on the flight across the ocean, and now, when *Cosmopolitan* magazine offered her a post as Aviation Editor, she accepted quickly. She wrote a whole body of articles on the advantages of flying for women, stating her own convictions clearly and strongly. She answered thousands of letters from readers, always stressing one point — that flying was important, that it was exciting, that it was worth the time it took and the inevitable element of risk. Flying, always her greatest love, was becoming a monumental passion with her. It dominated her completely and drove her on to ever greater tests of her own capability.

Her own flying became progressively more important and adventurous. She had never tried racing before; now, in 1929, she entered the first Women's Air Derby from Santa Monica, California, to Cleveland, Ohio, an eight-day race which newsmen instantly dubbed the Powder Puff Derby — a name which has lasted to the present time. In a new plane, a Lockheed Vega, Amelia completed the grueling flight that claimed one woman's life and saw more than a few planes crack up and drop out of competition. Amelia took third place.

Speed interested her now and she began trying for records. In November, she set a woman's speed record for a one-mile flight, and in July of 1930, she established a woman's record for a three-mile course, flying at 181 miles per hour.

Amelia pursued one interest after another, all of them linked with aviation. She took a job with an airline, traveling across the country to lecture to women's groups on the value of flight. Women were afraid to go up in commercial planes, and the airlines knew that they must change this attitude if they were to be commercially successful. When women had the chance to see Amelia Earhart in person and to hear her point out the safety and pleasure of flying, many of them were convinced.

In 1931, the autogiro was developed, a forerunner of the modern helicopter. Amelia got a chance to test out the odd little machine. She flew it to 18,000 feet, setting an autogiro altitude record, and then took the time to fly it across the country and back again as part of a publicity stunt.

She had come along quickly in the few years since Bill Stultz had flown her across the ocean. Step by step, she had gone through the long course of growing into her fame until she was ready for the last step of all. It was something she had to do — something that had seemed necessary the moment she had stepped out of the three-motored *Friendship* and into the public eye.

She was going to fly the Atlantic again. But this time she would do it alone.

On May 20, 1932, just five years to the day after Charles Lindbergh had embarked on his historic flight, Amelia Earhart soloed in his wake. Her plane was a Lockheed Vega, a secondhand airplane with a new engine bought especially for the occasion. She hopped from Teterboro Airport, near Passaic, New Jersey, to Newfoundland, stopped for just a day, and took off in the early evening to make her try over the Atlantic.

Later that night things began to go wrong. Clouds built up and a storm broke, with lightning slashing near the plane and rain and sleet lashing its wings and fuselage. Amelia climbed, fighting to pull the plane up above the storm.

The wings iced up. The altimeter went out first, and after

that the tachometer was ruined by ice. Once, the plane spun crazily out of control, its balance ruined by ice on one wing. The little Vega was within a hundred feet of the waters below before she could pull it up out of the dive.

That night was a nightmare. Her exhaust manifold vibrated madly; her reserve gas tank split and began leaking gasoline. The morning sun failed to melt the ice from the Vega's wings, and Amelia realized she could not duplicate Lindbergh's flight completely. She had originally planned to shoot for Paris; now she changed her mind and decided to set the plane down in Britain.

Amelia was flying with a minimum of instruments, with a plane in poor condition. But she kept going, spotted land, circled carefully and smoothly set the plane down in a pasture.

She landed in Northern Ireland. She unbuckled her belt and stepped down from the cockpit. Frightened cows watched her from the far end of the green pasture. She took a deep breath, then reached up to pat the hull of the Vega.

She had done it. Four years before, she had become famous overnight for lying down while a man piloted her across the ocean. This time there had been no man to do the flying; there had been no one in the plane but Amelia herself. She would go down in history not only as the first woman to fly the Atlantic but the first to fly it solo.

She was famous all over again, but now she could relax and enjoy her fame. She knew that she had earned it.

There were always new challenges. Amelia was a leader now, the nation's foremost female flier and the equal of male pilots as well. She had sought supremacy in the three tests of flying ability — altitude, distance and speed. Now she would set out to break some records.

217

A few months after her solo flight across the ocean, she flew from Los Angeles to Newark in a little over 19 hours to set a transcontinental speed record for women. Less than a year later, she broke her own record by knocking two full hours off her flying time.

In 1935, she became the first person to fly solo from Hawaii to the United States mainland. That same year, she made the first solo flight from Los Angeles to Mexico City; from Mexico City she made a record flight to Newark.

There were awards, there was publicity, there was acclaim. Her fame never diminished, because she never slowed down the pace. Purdue University added her to its faculty, to help younger women make the most of their opportunities, not only in aviation but in every field of human endeavor.

Amelia went on speaking and writing articles and giving interviews. Most important of all, she went on flying. She had come a long way from that fairground in Des Moines where she had had her first look at a plane; and her attitude toward aviation had changed a great deal since her ninth birthday. Then she had preferred paper hats and pony rides to airplanes; now flying was everything to her — challenge and reward at once. She met each challenge as it came and took each reward with grace.

Her last challenge was the world.

Men had flown around the world before — Wiley Post had done it twice — but no pilot, man or woman, had succeeded in flying around the globe at the Equator. That would be the ultimate triumph, Amelia thought. It would be her last flight and her most important one. She would fly farther than anyone had ever flown before and she would do something no one had ever done before.

Then, perhaps, she would quit flying. She was almost

thirty-nine, and every added year was important to a pilot. Reflexes began to slow down and timing was not as good as it had been, once a flier started to age. A flight around the world would be the perfect finale to her career.

She probably would have gone on flying, though. It was in her blood. Once she circled the globe, she would have continued to look for new worlds to conquer in the air. But this flight around the world was to be her last. It was the one from which she never returned.

The story of Amelia Earhart's final flight, filled with problems, is shrouded in mystery. Her plane left Oakland Airport in California on Saint Patrick's Day, 1937, with Fred Noonan aboard as navigator. She flew to Honolulu, then cracked up her plane on takeoff. Two months later, she was ready to try again, this time flying eastward instead of west. For a month and for 22,000 miles, Amelia and Noonan kept up the grueling pace. Finally, on June 30th, they took off from New Guinea. Their next landing place was to be Howland Island.

They never reached it. Somewhere between New Guinea and Howland, their Electra went down. Amelia Earhart vanished forever. She was never seen again.

What happened? Probably no one will ever know for certain. A sea of rumors has sprung up over the years: that she and Noonan were drowned; that they were captured by the Japanese; that they were stranded on an uninhabited island somewhere in the Pacific. The best evidence presently available suggests that Amelia was forced to crashland on the island of Saipan, where she and Fred Noonan were executed by Japanese soldiers.

But even this explanation is a guess at best. The world cannot say with certainty what happened to Amelia Earhart. Her disappearance remains one of the classic mysteries of the twentieth century, and one which may never be solved.

However the end came, the world has no trouble in assessing the place of this attractive young woman in the history of American aviation. She loved the world of flight and labored to prove herself worthy of that world. She proved at once the possibilities of the airplane and the courage of American womanhood. A modest person, she shrugged off fame even as she went out of her way to make herself worthy of it. When it was thrust suddenly upon her after her first transoceanic flight, she was only spurred on to outdo her own accomplishments.

In a sense, the final tragedy of her disappearance in the Pacific was almost inevitable. No victory was enough for Amelia Earhart. Each triumph only made her more anxious to test herself again. Nothing seemed to frighten her; no crash bothered her enough to make her leave the air for safer ground.

She always made light of her own accomplishments. "I hope this flight advances aviation," she said after her solo crossing of the Atlantic. "But I'll be very much surprised if it does." She went to great lengths to avoid exaggerating her own importance to the rest of the world. She might be proud of her aeronautical feats, but she refused to over-emphasize their value to the public as a whole.

Yet the greatest value of Amelia Earhart lay not so much in the importance of her flying — her speed and distance records — as it did in Amelia Earhart herself. This young woman, courageous and self-sufficient, determined and resourceful, was indeed an epitome of the ideal woman of her generation. She was an inspiration to men and women both. She remains one to this day.

CLARENCE DARROW
Lawyer

The courtroom in Los Angeles was jammed to overflowing that April morning in 1912. Men fought in an effort to get inside, and police were finally summoned to hold back the mob. Everyone wanted to be in on the show. Clarence Darrow, the nation's leading trial lawyer, had made history with his brilliant speeches in defense of his own clients. Now he would speak in his own defense, employing his own skill with words in a desperate bid to save himself from prison and disgrace.

Darrow had come to California to defend James and John McNamara, two labor leaders accused of dynamiting the Los Angeles Times Building and killing twenty men in the process. Public opinion was strong against the McNamaras, but Darrow had made a reputation for defending unpopular clients. Socialist leaders like Eugene V. Debs, labor organizers like Big Bill Haywood, Charles Moyer and George Pettibone — these and other men owed their freedom to Darrow's pleading in their behalf. Powerful business interests were allied against the McNamara brothers, and Darrow was convinced that they were being framed.

But his opinions changed as he prepared for trial. He came to the conclusion that the McNamaras were guilty and that it would be impossible to get them acquitted, and he succeeded, in turn, in showing the brothers that their best course lay in changing their plea to guilty in order to escape the death penalty. They agreed, and at this point Darrow had thought that the case was over.

Then, unexpectedly, he was charged with attempting to bribe a juror. The prosecution rounded up a batch of witnesses who were prepared to testify for the State and against Darrow. The charge was a serious one, and the full injustice of it struck the brilliant lawyer with the force of a sledgehammer blow. He engaged Earl Rogers, the most brilliant criminal lawyer in the West, to handle his case. Then he sat back, stunned, as the trial proceeded.

Now, on the final day of the trial, Darrow motioned Rogers aside and got slowly to his feet. The shock of the bribery charge had worn off, leaving in its place a firm determination to win freedom and reputation.

Darrow was a tall man, his shoulders slightly stooped, his sharp eyes set deep in his lined face. He was fifty-five years old, and all of these years showed in his eyes and his stance. He stood for a moment, his thumbs hooked under his suspenders, his eyes on the twelve jurors. Then, slowly and haltingly, he began to speak.

"I am on trial," he told the jury, "because I have been a lover of the poor, a friend of the oppressed; because I have stood by labor for all these years, and have brought down

222

upon my head the wrath of the criminal interests in this country."

Clarence Darrow spoke without pause for three full hours. He did more than smash the prosecution's case against him — he presented a powerful argument for himself and for the life he had led. Jurors and spectators wept before he was through. The jury took just thirty-four minutes to vote a verdict of Not Guilty, and the crowd in the courtroom rose to its feet and applauded. Darrow was a free man.

And yet he thought of himself as a beaten man. Guilty or not guilty, the bribery charge had been a tremendous smear on his reputation. He had left his Chicago law firm when he undertook the defense of the McNamaras. Now his good name had been sullied, his professional opportunities dimmed. The expenses of the trial had drained his resources and left him in debt. In his own eyes he was finished. He went back to Chicago with his wife Ruby, bleakly certain that the future held no promise for him.

Darrow could hardly have been more mistaken. Instead of sinking into obscurity, he rose to greater fame and prominence than he had ever known before. Instead of spending his remaining years idly, he kept busy throughout the Twenties, pleading one vital case after the next, spearheading unpopular causes and defending — and freeing — men who seemed hopelessly doomed. Instead of retiring to lick his wounds, Darrow went on to make his mark as the foremost lawyer in America's history.

Even as a boy, Clarence Darrow had known that he was a little different from other people. He grew up in Kinsman, Ohio, and everyone in that town thought of the Darrows as a little odd. Clarence's father Amirus was a dreamy idealist who spent his time with books while his family lived in poverty. The folks in Kinsman didn't care much for Amirus Darrow's opinions, either. He disagreed with accepted views of religion, held radical notions about politics and economics and government, and did not hesitate to speak his mind.

As a boy, Clarence learned how to argue. He learned how to say what he meant and, just as important, he knew how to bring people around to his way of thinking. It was almost inevitable that he would choose the legal profession. The idea of standing up in court to argue a case was irresistible to him.

At seventeen, Clarence was teaching grade school in Kinsman. By then he had made up his mind to be a lawyer. He saved his money for three years, borrowed from his older brother Everett, and finally spent a year at a law school in Ann Arbor, Michigan. That one year's study, plus another year of clerking for a lawyer in a nearby town, was as much training as Darrow had. He took the bar examination, passed it, and was authorized to practice law in Ohio.

He opened a law office in Andover, married a girl named Jessie, and worked hard at his practice. Business was slow at first, but little by little it grew. Three years later, Darrow and his wife moved to Ashtabula, where he was offered a minor city government post and where he had a better opportunity to build a profitable practice.

He did well in Ashtabula. His natural love for a good argument made trial law a perfect profession for him, and his deep interest in good books and new philosophies gave him a depth which other local lawyers lacked. In addition, Darrow knew how to aim his argument at the men and women in the jurors' box. While his opponents bored jurors to sleep with a sea of heretofores and whereases, Darrow mastered the knack of creating a sound, logical argument and presenting it so that the average person could follow it with interest.

As the years passed, Darrow found himself easily drifting into the comfortable life of a moderately successful small-town lawyer. His wife gave birth to a son. Darrow had money saved and thought seriously about buying a house for his growing family, but something held him back. He felt a need for a more demanding way of life than the one he had found in Ashtabula. He was reading a great deal, becoming interested in political and economic questions, and there was no one in Ashtabula to discuss these with him.

His work, too, left something to be desired. Legal argument for its own sake was not enough; he wanted to be concerned with more burning questions than disagreements over the ownership of a farm animal or questions of title to an abandoned shack.

After five years in Ashtabula, Darrow made his decision, quickly and firmly. He closed his law office, resigned his post with the city, and moved to Chicago. He had no prospects there, no important contacts, nothing but his own determination.

The furious hustle of Chicago in the later years of the nineteenth century made a sharp contrast with Ashtabula. Young Clarence Darrow was immediately drawn into the furious intellectual life of the city. He spent his days waiting for business in a tiny one-room law office, but his nights were given up to meetings and debates throughout Chicago. One night he would speak on the problem of poverty and the rights of working men to organize into unions; the next would find him debating socialist and anarchist doctrines. He could and would take any side of any argument, but his own feelings were developing and his own career was being shaped in the process.

Though he tried few cases at first, his nighttime activities were making him famous. A bristling speech at the Henry

George Club led to an appointment as Assessment Attorney for the city of Chicago. Later he moved up to Assistant Corporation Counsel. He put on weight, his features grew firm, and his voice took on unquestionable authority. When the Chicago and Northwestern Railway hired him as their general attorney, his future seemed assured. Corporation work, as everyone knew, was the ideal slot for a lawyer with ability.

But Clarence Darrow had been born to be the spokesman for the underdog, the defender of the underprivileged. He saw men working twelve and fourteen hours a day for subsistence wages, saw labor unions crushed by corrupt politicians acting at the behest of powerful business interests. He understood the only course that was open to him — the only course that would permit him to go on living with a clear conscience.

In 1895, Darrow represented Eugene V. Debs. Debs had been charged with conspiracy for organizing the Pullman workers' strike, and the idea of a railroad lawyer taking the workers' side was unprecedented. But Darrow took the case, unwilling to see injustice triumph. It was a clear-cut issue, as far as he could see. When the railway men formed an association, it was legal; when the workers did the same thing, the law called it a conspiracy.

Darrow handled Debs's defense in a way that would become his trademark. Instead of attacking the evidence against Debs — instead of denying the prosecution's charges — Darrow turned the tables and put the railroads themselves on the defensive. He attacked the law itself, using the courtroom as a forum designed not only to free Debs and his fellow defendants but to change public opinion throughout the nation.

The trial was not entirely a success for Darrow. A juror's

illness led to a mistrial, and the charges were dropped; later, Debs was brought before a judge on another count and sentenced to six months in jail. But Darrow was off on the course he was to follow for the rest of his life. Later, he defended the leaders of a woodworkers' union in a similar case of conspiracy and proceeded in the same fashion. Instead of denying the charges, he put the employer on trial by exposing his treatment of his workers. Darrow's final plea to the jury was a masterpiece of the sort he became famous for, a brilliant, logical and highly emotional plea for acquittal. This time he won a clear-cut victory and the union leaders were acquitted.

In case after case, Darrow took the side of the underdog and fought for causes in which he believed. In 1902, he represented the United Mine Workers at a hearing and won them the right to represent their workers in bargaining sessions with employers. Five years later, he traveled to Idaho to defend Big Bill Haywood, Charles Moyer and George Pettibone. The three men, leaders of the Western Federation of Miners, were charged with murder.

The case was a frame-up and Darrow realized it. Union men and mine owners had been in armed conflict in the West for years, and either side was willing to go to any lengths to destroy the other. When a petty thief named Harry Orchard killed the former Governor of Idaho with a homemade bomb, the mine owners decided to capitalize on the crime. They persuaded Orchard to testify that Haywood and the other union leaders had put him up to it. The charges were ridiculous, but the mine owners had powerful allies in the Idaho government, and it looked as though the three defendants would be found guilty. They had been kidnaped from Colorado illegally and returned to Idaho for trial.

The prosecution decided to bring them to trial one at a

time, with Haywood leading off. Darrow took a train to Boise, Idaho, and worked to establish a defense. At first, his hands were tied because Orchard's charges were completely false and it was impossible for him to guess what alibi he could establish for Haywood.

Then Darrow got a lucky break. Harry Orchard had been kept in seclusion since his arrest. Suddenly he was allowed to meet with newspapermen, and the self-proclaimed killer proceeded to outline the prosecution's entire case for the press. Darrow couldn't believe his luck. Through incredibly hard work, he was able to build his defense so that an iron-clad alibi was established for Haywood.

The trial represented an all-out triumph for Darrow and his clients: the prosecution's case was smashed; Harry Orchard himself was exposed as a liar and his testimony utterly discredited. And, in his summation to the jury, Darrow turned the tables in his usual style and thundered against the men responsible for framing Haywood in the first place. The trial itself had lasted eleven weeks; Darrow's closing speech lasted eleven full hours. Once again he was speaking not only to the twelve men who sat on the jury — he was speaking to the nation.

Haywood was acquitted. Pettibone's trial followed and he, too, was acquitted. Charges against the remaining man, Moyer, were dropped.

Darrow went on defending the innocent, championing unpopular causes, fighting for the things in which he believed. He made speeches and took part in debates. He opposed capital punishment, argued against religious bigotry, criticized the exploitive elements of capitalism. Many people denounced him, but a great many others listened to him.

Then came the McNamara case, and Darrow's own trial for bribery. After his acquittal, he was in Chicago once more, a middle-aged man with stooped shoulders and keen eyes, a man quite thoroughly convinced that the glory of his life was behind him.

Slowly, step by step, Clarence Darrow began to realize that his professional life was by no means over. He was in constant demand as a lecturer, and the public swarmed to hear and applaud him. A pair of Chicago lawyers invited him to join their firm. He began to try cases once again, and he never ceased to win them.

Brilliance in law is not rare among lawyers. But a trial lawyer, to be effective, must have a flair for the dramatic, a keen understanding of human psychology, and an ability to make his point clearly and directly. Darrow was a master of all the tricks of courtroom law, from the subtlest to the most electrifying.

A favorite gambit of his was designed to destroy the force of a prosecuting attorney's argument without Darrow having to say a word. He simply inserted a length of wire in a cigar and smoked it while his opponent launched into his speech. The hidden wire kept the ash from falling. The ash grew longer and longer until the attention of every juror was riveted, not to the District Attorney's argument but to the incredible ash on Clarence Darrow's cigar. However forceful the prosecutor's logic, it had little chance of making an impression upon the jury.

But tricks alone were not enough to make Darrow great. In addition to his grasp of legal technique, he had a deep conviction of right and wrong and the willingness to back his convictions to the hilt. It was said that he always managed to believe in his clients and in his cases. This made a forcible impression upon jurymen. It is hard to disregard the impassioned plea of a man who is totally committed to his cause.

Darrow did believe in his clients, and the juries were persuaded to do likewise.

When World War I ended in 1918, the country found itself in the grip of what has come to be called the Red Scare. A Communist revolution had overthrown the Czar's regime in Russia, and many people had become convinced that America was menaced by Communism and that any and all means should be used to counteract this threat. State after state passed laws which violated the free speech provision of the Constitution. Radical politicians of every description were rounded up in wholesale lots and tossed into jail on the flimsiest of pretexts. They were charged, not with having *done* specific acts but with having *advocated* radical policies. In short, they were being imprisoned for their thoughts rather than for their actions.

All of this infuriated Clarence Darrow. His sense of justice rebelled at the idea of any man being thrown in jail as a consequence of his beliefs. In 1920, twenty members of the Communist Labor Party of Chicago were brought to trial on charges of "advocating the violent overthrow of the Government."

Darrow defended them.

Some people could not understand his action. The defendants had opposed America's entrance into the war, while Darrow himself had urged American intervention from the day Belgium had been invaded by the German armies.

Darrow answered their objections in his summation:

When I entered the practice of my profession, I determined that there would never be a case, however unpopular, where I would refuse to do my duty to defend that case. I have never turned my back upon any defendant, no matter what the charge. When the cry is the loudest the defendant needs the lawyer most; when every other man has turned against him the law provides that he should have a lawyer.

He went on, defending not only his clients but the principles of free speech and free thought, attacking not only the State's case but the unconstitutional law under which the twenty men had been brought to trial. The case itself was a hopeless one; public opinion had convicted Darrow's clients long before the trial had begun. But once again Darrow was speaking to the entire nation over the heads of the jury.

His summary speech was a classic affirmation of the American principles of freedom and civil liberties. The jury found the twenty men guilty — no other verdict was possible since they had violated the unconstitutional law under which they were being tried. On appeal, the Illinois Supreme Court upheld the conviction.

On the surface, it looked like a defeat for Darrow, but his brilliant pleading had started ripples below the ground. One Supreme Court Justice wrote a dissenting opinion upholding the principles for which Darrow had argued. The Governor of Illinois pardoned the defendants before they began to serve their sentences. And the landslide of public opinion began to shift in another direction. The Red Scare lost impetus, and Americans once again began to show that their nation had been founded upon the precept of freedom for all men, even for those who opposed some of the basic principles of American democracy.

If Darrow had made himself unpopular by defending the Communist Labor Party members, he did far more to arouse public opinion against himself four years later. In 1920, he had defended twenty men whose political opinions were sharply at odds with those of the rest of society. In 1924, he defended two young boys who had committed a crime that shocked and sickened the entire nation.

Richard Loeb and Nathan Leopold were the teen-age sons of two of Chicago's wealthiest families. They were brilliant boys. Each was the youngest student ever graduated from his respective college. Carried away by weird philosophy and by their own mad fantasies, the two boys decided to see if they could commit "the perfect crime."

They kidnaped a boy named Bobby Franks, the fourteen-year-old son of a Chicago businessman. They murdered the boy in cold blood and attempted to collect ransom money from his parents. Their venture was hardly the perfect crime they had planned. On the contrary, they left a trail a mile wide. Both boys were quickly caught; both quickly confessed.

The city of Chicago was jolted by the crime. Newspapers screamed for vengeance, demanding the blood of Leopold and Loeb. When Darrow himself agreed to undertake their defense, the public outrage defied description. In the eyes of most Chicagoans, the great wealth of the two families was being used to purchase the lives of two contemptible killers. Everyone took it for granted that Darrow was defending the boys for a staggering fee, that he was selling out for the high price that the Leopolds and the Loebs could pay him.

Clarence Darrow had never sold out, and this case was no exception. When he had first come to Chicago from Ashtabula, a book by Illinois Governor John Peter Altgeld had influenced his views on capital punishment, and these views had deepened and strengthened with the passage of time. Darrow was convinced that capital punishment was profoundly wrong, that it was an evil which accomplished nothing. It did not dissuade anyone from committing murder, but only made a man pay with his own life for the life he had taken.

In short, it made murderers of every member of society.

Feeling as he did, Darrow could hardly turn down the defense of Leopold and Loeb. And he saw that he could use this case as a forum for his own views on capital punishment. The boys had confessed, there was no question of their going free, and Darrow had no intention of pressing for an acquittal. He only wanted to save their lives and establish a precedent for the saving of future lives.

Everyone expected Darrow to plead the boys insane; with all his legal skill, they felt he might manage to make an insanity plea stand up. The lawyer studied psychology day and night, saturated himself in every aspect of the case. He came to the conclusion that the boys were not insane and that it would be impossible to save them with such a plea.

Instead, Darrow took a brand new course. He argued that the youth of the boys, their emotional immaturity, their fantasies, all combined to create circumstances which demanded mercy from the law. His whole argument was for not justice but mercy. While he did not plead them insane, he argued that they were not "in their right minds" when they planned and executed their crime.

"Why did they kill little Bobby Franks?" he demanded. And he answered himself, "They killed him because they were made that way. Because somewhere in the infinite processes that go to the making up of the boy or the man something slipped, and those unfortunate lads sit here hated, despised outcasts, with the community shouting for their blood."

There was no jury for Darrow to sway this time. He had to aim his plea at a single man, the Chief Justice of the Criminal Court of Cook County. It was not enough to move the judge emotionally; Darrow had to do more. He had to make this man see that mercy was not only deserved but legally desirable.

Darrow fought to save the lives of Leopold and Loeb. He never tried to win their freedom. "I know that these boys are not fit to be at large," he said. "They will not be until they pass through the next stage of life at forty-five or fifty. Whether they will be then, I cannot tell."

When Darrow finished his final speech on behalf of the two boys, tears were streaming down the judge's face, and the overcrowded courtroom held its breath to a man. His final plea, a speech which lasted over twelve hours, was reproduced in full in many newspapers throughout the country.

In September of 1924, Nathan Leopold and Richard Loeb were sentenced to life imprisonment with an additional ninety-year sentence for kidnaping. Clarence Darrow had done what he had set out to do. He had saved their lives.

The Leopold–Loeb case was the ultimate in dramatic tragedy. The Scopes case, which Darrow defended a year later in 1925, came almost as comic relief. If that "Monkey Trial," as it was called, had not possessed such far-reaching significance, and if it had not touched so many people so deeply, it would have appeared as a classic example of legal comedy.

The State of Tennessee, like many other states throughout the country, had passed a law forbidding the teaching in the schools of any theory that appeared to contradict the Bible. If enforced, the law would effectively prevent the teaching of a whole body of scientific knowledge. Not only the theory of evolution, but knowledge of all scientific advances that seemed to disagree with the Biblical story of creation would be proscribed for children in schools.

John Scopes, a schoolteacher in Dayton, Tennessee,

agreed to test the law. He taught evolution in his classes. Friends of his reported him to the local authorities, and Scopes was indicted.

In no time at all, the case became a battlefield for the forces of fundamentalist religion and the advocates of educational freedom. William Jennings Bryan, three times a defeated candidate for the Presidency, took the side of the prosecution. And Darrow, always a champion of the rights of progress and science, volunteered his services for the defense.

But in a sense Darrow did not defend Scopes at all. Scopes had gone out of his way to admit his "guilt" in breaking the antievolution law. Darrow was intent upon using the case to attack a law he thought unjust and unconstitutional, and he used the little courtroom in the small town of Dayton to pave the way so that this law itself could be struck down on appeal.

People came from all over the country to watch the show. Dayton became a haven for tourists and curiosity seekers overnight. The spectacle centered on the dynamic personalities of two men — Bryan for the prosecution; Clarence Darrow for the defense.

Darrow was not an enemy of religion, but he had long opposed the excesses of orthodox religion and the abuses which such religion could create. A lifelong student of the Bible, he used his familiarity with the Scriptures to strike out against the folly of taking the Bible too literally. In a brilliant display of legal showmanship, the old lawyer put Bryan himself on the witness stand and cross-examined him at length, reading the Bible to him and dramatically showing that a strict view of its contents was out of place in the modern world. He challenged Bryan to agree that the world had been created in six days and that Joshua had literally made the sun stand still.

By the time Darrow had finished, Bryan himself had broken down to admit his own confusion. Again and again Darrow made his point — that any man who took the Bible word for word was rejecting all the advances of modern science, and that such a restriction could cripple the schools of the country.

Scopes was found guilty and fined $100. This was a foregone conclusion, for Darrow himself had requested a verdict of guilty so that the law itself could be appealed to a higher court. The State Supreme Court set aside Scopes's conviction on a technicality but upheld the law itself. It didn't matter. Darrow had destroyed the law for all practical purposes, smashing it with the force of his words. While the law might remain on the books, evolution would be taught in the public schools.

In 1926, Clarence Darrow once again found himself defending a client charged with murder, and once again the case seemed to center upon more than the legal questions involved. This time the defendants were Dr. Ossian Sweet and his brother Henry. Dr. Sweet, a successful Negro physician, had purchased a home in a white neighborhood in Detroit. An unruly white mob attacked his house, jeering at the Sweets and hurling rocks through the windows. To protect their lives and their property, the Sweets fired several shots over the heads of the mob. In the uproar, two men were shot. One died, and the Sweets were charged with murder.

From a legal standpoint, the case should have been a simple one for Darrow. Dr. Sweet had been within his rights in protecting his home and his family. Besides, there was no way to prove whether the dead man had been shot by Sweet or by the police who had attempted to disperse the mob of angry men. But once again Darrow was confronted not so much by the law as by the mass of public opinion. It was prejudice that was calling for the lives of Ossian and Henry Sweet.

Clarence Darrow had long been a friend of the Negroes. His own father had worked with the Underground Railway to smuggle runaway slaves into Canada before the Civil War. Darrow himself, a fiercely independent man who had stubbornly refused to join any political organization, had broken this rule to join the National Association for the Advancement of Colored People. And, in the pattern that had become a familiar one by now, he proceeded to defend the Sweets by attacking the very roots of prejudice.

He lectured the jury on the history of the Negro people in America. He lashed out at the climate of opinion that could place a man like Dr. Ossian Sweet on trial for his life. In a seven-hour closing speech, Darrow chose words and arguments that reached every member of the jury. He won his case; the Sweets went free. And he struck another significant blow in his war against prejudice and hate.

By the time the Twenties were over, Clarence Darrow was an old man. He had lived a long life and had been busy every minute of it, devoting himself completely to the causes that seemed just to him. He had tried to retire several times. Then time after time he had come back into the ring as some new problem demanded his attention.

In 1932, he went to Hawaii to defend a man charged with murder. He won the case. During the early years of the Roosevelt Administration, he accepted a Presidential appointment to investigate the workings of the National Recovery Act.

Retirement, when it finally did come, could not mean a time of doing nothing. Clarence Darrow was unable to sit around. He had to keep busy. He delivered lectures and wrote his autobiography. He was a man who loved life, and he squeezed every possible bit of activity out of it.

In 1938, at the age of eighty-one, Clarence Darrow died. His death came a full twenty-six years after his bribery trial in Los Angeles, more than a quarter of a century after Darrow had thought of himself as finished. He had gone on to greater and greater glory, and when he died, a whole nation mourned his passing. No other lawyer had ever captured the spirit of his country as completely as Darrow had. In the years that followed his death, his reputation has grown until his name has become a fiery symbol of legal courage and brilliance.

GEORGE GERSHWIN
Composer

The year was 1908, and the boy playing ball in a school-yard on New York's tumultuous Lower East Side was just ten years old. He was an all-around boy, the best roller skater on the block, a topnotch marble shooter. But now, as he cocked his arm to throw the ball, something caught him and gripped him. It was music — the haunting strains of Dvořák's "Humoresque" filtering out through an open window of the school.

Someone tossed the ball back to him. The boy stepped aside, letting it bounce past him. "Count me out," he said. "I've got something to do."

He moved to the open window and stayed there, hypnotized by the music of the violinist within. Later he managed to meet the boy who had played the violin so beautifully. The boy was Maxie Rosenzweig — in later years he would become famous as concert violinist Max Rosen.

Under Maxie's guidance, the young boy became drawn into the world of good music. He began teaching himself to play the piano at a friend's home. In school, he would gaze out the window and tap out tunes of his own on the top of his desk. He even tried writing songs of his own, and these he showed to Maxie.

But the violinist's reaction was a discouraging one. "You just haven't got it in you to become a musician," Maxie told him. "You can take my word for it. I know."

The boy didn't listen, and it was a good thing that he didn't. Eleven years later he would write a song called "Swanee," one of the all-time popular hits. And before long he would emerge as the leading musical spirit of the Jazz Age, with his name and his tunes on the lips of the nation.

While George Gershwin found both fame and riches in life, his childhood promised neither. His father Morris had come to America in the early 1890's. Morris' own father, a mechanic, had served in the Czar's Army for twenty-five years, beginning at the age of ten. It seemed as though he was destined to follow in his footsteps, since this was the fate of almost every able-bodied man in Russia.

But Morris slipped away to America. His uncle was a tailor in New York City, and Morris turned to him for aid. In 1895, Morris married Rose Bruskin, a girl he had known in Russia. A year later Ira was born. Two years after that, while the Gershwins were living in Brooklyn, George was born. Shortly thereafter the family moved across the river to the Lower East Side of Manhattan, where they remained for twenty years. Morris Gershwin turned from one business to another, never hitting bottom but never breaking through to real success. He served as foreman of a shoe factory, managed a Turkish bath, and tried his hand at many ventures.

The neighborhood where George grew up was a perfect illustration of the idea of America as a melting pot. Immigrants from a dozen countries thronged its narrow streets. Women chattered in countless Eastern European languages and dialects. Horse-drawn wagons clattered along its cobble-stone streets, with vendors crying out their wares at the top of their lungs. When an elevated subway train roared by overhead, the vibrations rattled windows in the tenement buildings on either side.

There was little in those early years to indicate that George had any particular musical ability. He threw himself whole-heartedly into the furious activities of the neighborhood — punch ball, street hockey, stickball and stoopball. With a broom handle for a bat and a manhole cover serving as home plate, he and his friends fitted their games to the conditions of city living.

In school, George got into trouble frequently. He was a bright boy but his high spirits often led to mischief and there were many days when he never got around to doing his homework.

But a deep love for music was buried somewhere inside him, and now and then it would come to the surface. When he was six, he heard Anton Rubenstein's "Melody in F" played on an automatic piano in a penny arcade. The tune made a lasting impression on him. Later he recalled, "The peculiar jumps in the music held me rooted. To this day I can't hear the tune without picturing myself standing outside that arcade."

And later, on a roller-skating expedition to Harlem, he happened to pass a jazz club while Jim Europe's band was playing. The harsh, strident tones of this new music were a revelation to him, and he returned to the spot frequently, spending hours on the sidewalk listening to blues, ragtime and spirituals. All of these elements — classical music, jazz, blues, and above all the sounds of the modern city itself — were later to be recognizable as characteristics of Gershwin's music.

In 1910, two years after Maxie Rosenzweig's rendition of "Humoresque" had awakened George's interest in music once and for all, the boy's musical career took a giant step forward when the Gershwin family bought a piano. As soon as the bulky piano had been hoisted through a window and set down in the cluttered living room, George's life was changed permanently. He sat down at once and began pounding out a tune, awkwardly and in octaves. Outside, the sounds of the bustling city went on, but George no longer heard them. All he could hear were the songs he played and the other new melodies that began to grow in his mind.

Although the piano had been bought for George's older brother Ira, it was George who began taking lessons. He studied with several local teachers, then, in 1912, was accepted as a pupil by Charles Hambitzer. It was Hambitzer, a fine musician, who was the first to recognize young Gershwin's tremendous talent. In a letter to his sister, Hambitzer referred to George as one who would make his mark in music. "The boy is a genius, without a doubt," Hambitzer wrote. "He's crazy about music and can't wait until it's time to take his lessons."

George could not have found a better teacher. Not content to give George only classical music, Hambitzer made him familiar with the world of modern composers and schooled him in harmony, theory and instrumentation. But Hambitzer could not help being upset by George's continuing interest in popular music. As far as the teacher was concerned, popular songs were nothing but a waste of time.

But even then, George realized that popular music could serve as the wellspring for a successful American musical tradition. He tried to convince Hambitzer of this — tried to show the older man the value of joining the harmonic techniques of classical music with the melody and rhythm of popular themes. Hambitzer remained unconvinced, but George had found his musical purpose.

At the time, the two fields of classical and popular music could hardly have been further apart. The jazz musicians of the day were for the most part musically uneducated: many of them could not even read music, much less arrange a score for a large-sized orchestra. The classical musicians, on the other hand, thought of jazz as nothing but chaotic noise. While a few European composers recognized jazz as valid music, many American composers did their best to ignore it.

George went on working in the two areas at once. He worked on his piano technique constantly and immersed himself in the theory of music. At the same time he began to concentrate on popular music. At the age of fifteen he wrote his first real song, "Since I Found You," which remained unpublished. The next year, he played the piano at an evening's entertainment sponsored by a literary club, playing a tango which he had composed himself.

It was about this time that George dropped out of school to take a job in Tin Pan Alley as a staff pianist and song plugger. His salary was only $15 a week, but he felt that the job would give him an opportunity to learn the popular music business from the ground up.

His parents opposed the move. "What future is there for you?" Rose Gershwin demanded. "You'll play the piano for twenty-five dollars a week for the rest of your life. You should continue your education, George. You should make something out of yourself."

Gershwin fully intended to make something of himself, and was convinced that he had found the right road to success. In his work in Tin Pan Alley, he met men like Irving Berlin and Jerome Kern, the leading popular composers of the day. George impressed people with his piano playing:

the song pluggers and writers of Tin Pan Alley were not accustomed to hearing a pianist with such a firm grasp of classical technique. And he went on writing songs. His first was published in 1916. That same year, another song of Gershwin's was heard on Broadway in *The Passing Show of 1916.*

George went from job to job, finding his way, always experimenting, always learning. He worked as a rehearsal pianist, as an arranger, and finally as a songwriter. This last job gave him the greatest opportunity to develop his talent. He was paid a flat salary of $35 a week to write songs for a publishing house. He set his own hours, wrote his own songs, and devoted full time to this work.

Most of the songs he wrote at this time were never published. Others landed in minor Broadway revues or found their way onto records, but none achieved any great success. This could have been a discouraging time, but George Gershwin was not easily discouraged. He was firmly convinced of his own ability and felt that it was only a question of time before the rest of the world would take notice of him.

In 1919, Gershwin got his first real taste of success. His song "Swanee," with lyrics by Irving Caesar, was introduced on Broadway by the great Al Jolson. It was an instant success. Stores all over the nation did a land-office business in the sheet music of "Swanee," as well as in Jolson's famous recording of the song. No other song that Gershwin was to write would ever equal the tremendous commercial success of "Swanee." It was the hit of the year and it has come down as a classic of popular music.

With such overnight success, it would have been easy enough for young George Gershwin to completely give himself up to the writing of popular hits. He did continue in this direction, but he revealed his tremendous technical skill in everything he wrote.

Between 1920 and 1924, Gershwin wrote all the music for the *George White Scandals,* showing in this popular work his great originality in the use of changing rhythms, meters and modulations. He continued to grow, both as a pianist and as a composer, and he never lost sight of his dream of fusing classical techniques with popular themes to produce a truly American type of serious music.

It was Paul Whiteman who paved the way for the full development of Gershwin's potential. Whiteman, one of the famous orchestra leaders of the day, planned to put on a concert of American music in New York. It was his idea that Gershwin should write a serious work based on jazz themes, to be performed by a full orchestra. Gershwin went to work, pouring everything he knew and felt into the composition. He worked at the piano until his hands were bloody from constant playing.

When the piece was finished, he presented it to Whiteman. The bandleader was uncertain about it. It seemed too long, too involved, too popular and too serious at once. But Gershwin overcame his objections, and his composition was performed by Whiteman's orchestra on February 12, 1924.

"Rhapsody in Blue" — that was the title Gershwin picked for his composition. It would be hard to find a more perfect musical summation of the Twenties. Gay and violent, flippant and strident, Gershwin's "Rhapsody in Blue" was the product of everything within him and everything he had experienced. It caught the precise flavor of New York in the era of flappers and hip flasks and speakeasies, an era in which New York and America reacted to the end of the World War with a furious pursuit of pleasure.

Paul Whiteman's doubts and fears were swept aside forever by the audience's reaction to Gershwin's music. Those listening to that premiere performance were caught in the grip of a kind of music that was entirely new to them. Their concentration never wavered; at the end, the entire hall was swept with applause for minutes on end.

The next day, newspaper critics added their voices to that of the crowd. "Rhapsody in Blue" was proclaimed as one of the most significant works in American music, and Gershwin was heralded as the most promising composer on the American scene. If "Swanee" had made Gershwin commercially successful overnight, "Rhapsody in Blue" made him an artistic success as well. He was a celebrity. His name, recently known only to those in the business, was echoed everywnere.

What sort of man was this George Gershwin?

He was attractive, with a warm personality and a sincere, engaging manner. He was tall and slender, with a long, handsome, sensitive face. His eyes were softly expressive.

But no one could accuse Gershwin of hiding his light under a bushel. He took his music seriously, and he was one of his own greatest fans. At parties in New York and Hollywood, he was always to be found at the piano, playing his own music. In such a setting the people who surrounded him bárely existed. Just as the sounds of the Lower East Side had vanished for him in the days when he had first begun studying music, so did the party sounds disappear for him the moment he began to play. His music was the only reality.

Like so many artists, Gershwin was both in love with his music and dissatisfied with it. It has been said of many composers that music was their whole life; this was certainly true in Gershwin's case. As a result, he gave the appearance of being totally preoccupied with himself. His complete absorption in his own music was often viewed as thorough egotism.

"How long will Gershwin's music last?" a man asked. And the answer that came back was Oscar Levant's, "As long as Gershwin is around to play it."

Levant, a virtuoso pianist with a reputation for devastating wit, was one of George's closest friends and one of the first to recognize the young composer's genius. "George," he demanded once, "if you had your life to live over, would you fall in love with yourself all over again?"

But jibes like this had no effect on Gershwin. It was his music that mattered to him, and nothing else seemed important. Once, speaking of his own folk opera, *Porgy and Bess*, he said, "The music is so marvelous I can't believe it." And when a friend told him a certain piece of music was wonderful, Gershwin's reaction was: "*Only* wonderful?"

When the first bloom of success begins to fade, many creative artists begin to worry that they will go stale. A writer may fear that his second book will be a disappointment in the light of his first; a composer may dread running out of musical ideas.

This problem never seemed to bother Gershwin. So complete was his absorption in music that his mind was always teeming with musical ideas. Song melodies flowed from him unceasingly, and newer and more exciting musical projects came to him constantly.

Once, when he discovered that he had lost a notebook containing material for at least forty songs, he refused to become upset. Where another composer might have grown depressed or angry, Gershwin simply shrugged off the loss. "I have too many other ideas for songs to worry about it," he told a friend.

The success of "Rhapsody in Blue" made Gershwin a famous and a wealthy man overnight. Whiteman's recording became a best-seller, and the composition itself was arranged for every possible combination of instruments and performed extensively on both sides of the Atlantic. George never attempted to rest on his laurels. He went on working, devoting himself to both popular music and more serious efforts.

His continuing interest in the former drew some critical comment. Some argued that Gershwin should not bother with popular music and show tunes, that such work was beneath him now. Gershwin knew better. It was his dual interest in popular and classical music that had made "Rhapsody in Blue" possible, and he refused to believe that writing popular tunes could impair the quality of his more serious music.

In 1924, the same year that "Rhapsody" was first performed, Gershwin wrote the music for *Lady, Be Good*, a Broadway show that starred Fred Astaire. This show contained a number of hits, including "Fascinating Rhythm," but it is most important because it marked the first full-scale collaboration between George and his brother Ira.

The two brothers had worked together on songs, but now they had begun a partnership which became a permanent one. Ira's talents as a lyricist perfectly complemented George's ability as a composer, and the two produced some of the finest songs of the Twenties and Thirties, writing scores of songs for the Broadway stage and for Hollywood.

But while he composed for shows like *Lady, Be Good, Tip-Toes* (1925), *Oh, Kay!* (1926), *Funny Face* (1927) and *Girl Crazy* (1930), Gershwin did not abandon his more serious work. He went on striving toward his goal, joining elements of serious and popular music to produce something that truly reflected his own personality and the world in which he lived.

His "Piano Concerto in F," one of his more obviously "classical" works, had its premiere in December of 1925 at Carnegie Hall. Gershwin himself played the piano, with Walter Damrosch conducting the New York Symphony Society Orchestra. "An American in Paris," a tone poem in which Gershwin made extensive use of jazz themes, was first performed in 1928. His "Second Rhapsody" and his "Cuban Overture" followed four years later.

248

So perfectly did Gershwin combine the popular and the classical elements in his music, that some of his work defied classification — a source of unending confusion to many of his critics. In a Broadway musical comedy of 1930, *Girl Crazy*, he introduced the song "I Got Rhythm," a tune with such an interesting and complex harmonic structure that it is still used as the foundation of a great many modern jazz compositions. And in 1934, he published his "Variations on I Got Rhythm for Piano and Orchestra." As far as Gershwin was concerned, one could draw no hard and fast line separating the popular and the serious. This was his feeling, and his own work proved the correctness of it.

After the success of "Rhapsody in Blue," Gershwin was always a celebrity, always supplied with money and highly admired, yet his career was by no means a matter of one success after another. His own stubborn insistence on writing whatever music he wanted to write created a certain amount of difficulty for him. It would have been easy to rest on his laurels, to cease growing as a musician; having found a formula for success, he could have gone on creating endless variations on that formula forever.

But George Gershwin was not that type of man. He had to grow, had to experiment, had to find his way. As a result, there were times when the critics deprecated some of his serious compositions, and there were times when his popular work failed to gain the approval of the general public. A 1925 operetta, *A Song of the Flame*, failed on the Broadway stage. A pair of 1933 musicals, *Pardon My English* and *Let 'Em Eat Cake*, were box-office flops.

Even *Porgy and Bess,* which Gershwin felt very deeply about, was by no means a success at the beginning. This folk opera represented a new concept both in music and in the theatre. A simple story revolving around the affairs of a Negro community in the mythical setting of Catfish Row, *Porgy and Bess* possesses at once a moving love story, a good deal of native American humor, a story line loaded with conflict and dramatic strength, and some of the most hauntingly beautiful melodies ever written.

In 1935, the show was a failure. Music critics were unwilling to accept a work of this sort as opera; the public, used to a diet of lighthearted musical comedy, rejected the tragic ending of the show and stayed away from the box office.

Perhaps the failure of *Porgy and Bess* drove Gershwin from the Broadway stage. In any event, he never wrote for Broadway again. In 1936, he and Ira returned to Hollywood, where they had worked five years earlier. They wrote the scores for three more movies, *Damsels In Distress, Shall We Dance?* and *The Goldwyn Follies.* Some of George's greatest songs were written in Hollywood, including tunes like "Nice Work if You Can Get It," "Love Walked In," "Our Love Is Here to Stay," "They Can't Take That Away From Me," and "A Foggy Day in London Town."

In Hollywood, Gershwin lived the life of a celebrity, secure in the admiration of a circle of close friends. Although he planned a variety of more serious projects for the future, the heavy work schedule that faced him, coupled with disappointment over the reception of *Porgy and Bess,* kept George concentrating on popular songs and scores instead of focusing his energies upon more extensive works. The Hollywood life was a distraction that kept a good many writers and composers from doing all they might have done. George took part in that life, but at the same time refused to slacken his working pace. He drove himself relentlessly, as though determined to produce all he possibly could in the time he had.

The constant pace of hard, brain-wracking work began to tell on Gershwin during those Hollywood years. More than once, he pushed himself past the breaking point and his health suffered. He should have forced himself to slow down, but his temperament was such that he simply had to compose. There was music in his mind that had to be worked out and written down — songs that demanded to be born. He went on working.

In 1937, while working on *The Goldwyn Follies* — his last motion picture — George Gershwin's health broke completely and he collapsed. At first, the collapse was thought to be due to overwork and nervous strain, but the situation proved to be far more complicated. On July 9th, Gershwin was rushed to Cedars of Lebanon Hospital for brain surgery. An exploratory examination revealed a tumor on a part of the brain which could not be touched surgically. Two days later, at the age of thirty-nine years, George Gershwin died in his sleep.

Many more songs remained unwritten, many more serious musical masterpieces he might have produced remained unborn. Gershwin, a man who had had the great fortune to reach success at so young an age, was struck by the tragedy — like Keats and Mozart — of having his career cut short at an early age.

It has been said that one of the key measurements of a man's greatness is how long his name and his works remain after he himself has gone. How long would George Gershwin's music last? The cynical answer to this question — that it would last so long as Gershwin was around to play it — suddenly became challenged with the young composer's death. How long *would* Gershwin's music last?

Often a man's work will be dismissed during his lifetime only to be rediscovered by the critics years or generations later. This was not the case with Gershwin's music. Although some critics were willing to pass him off as unimportant, the American public never lost interest in Gershwin. Those of his works which had been successful during his lifetime grew in favor in the years that followed; those which had not been well received while he lived became increasingly popular with the passage of time. Over the years, "Rhapsody in Blue" has been the most frequently performed serious composition by any American composer.

The fate of that "failure," *Porgy and Bess*, was even more dramatic. The folk-opera form which Gershwin introduced had been years ahead of its time, but eventually the critics and the public caught up with it. In the early Fifties, an American Negro company performed the opera on a worldwide tour and received tremendous acclaim throughout Europe and the Soviet Union. Dance orchestras and modern jazz groups recorded various interpretations of its music. Finally, in 1959 — twenty-four years after its original production — Samuel Goldwyn produced a motion-picture adaptation of *Porgy and Bess* that drew capacity crowds throughout the country.

"For twenty years now," one critic wrote, "people have been waiting for the world to forget George Gershwin. Every year his stature as an artist and innovator grows another notch. It's time we took notice of the very genuine merit of his music."

The final proof of Gershwin's success may be seen in his popular works, those countless songs he wrote for Broadway musical comedies and Hollywood movies. This was the work that made the critics so anxious to ignore him — the work his friends urged him to forget as being beneath his talents. They repeatedly had told him that his songs were a waste of his talent; popular songs would not live, they assured him.

Gershwin himself probably believed this. It's doubtful that

he expected his show tunes to endure for any length of time. He wrote them to entertain the public and for his own musical enjoyment. Much as he desired to create a musical monument that would endure beyond his own lifetime, he could not avoid writing those melodies that were so much a part of him.

But even these endure. An astonishingly high proportion of Gershwin's songs have survived the test of time, becoming a part of our American musical heritage. His beautiful melodies have become standards, the frequent choice of jazz musicians, dance orchestras, and singers. Songs like "The Man I Love," "Sweet and Low Down," "But Not For Me," "Embraceable You," "Someone to Watch Over Me" — these and a whole score of others have won a degree of success that would be enough to ensure Gershwin's place in the history of American music. A list of his songs reads like a catalogue of the high points of our popular music tradition.

No other composer spoke for a growing, bustling, devil-may-care America as unforgettably as George Gershwin. Its anxieties, its exuberance, its passions were underlined by his infectious rhythms. Its color and background were reflected in his harmonies. It has been said that he influenced the direction of modern music more profoundly than any single composer with the exception, perhaps, of Igor Stravinksy. Gershwin's music, so much a part of his own time, has equal significance in our own time as well.

George Gershwin died a tragically premature death, but the body of music which he left behind has lived and goes on living. Every year, still more Americans find themselves humming his tunes, tapping their feet to his rhythms, or listening in absorbed silence to the strident excitement of his "Rhapsody in Blue."

INDEX

254

INDEX

INDEX

The Author

REX LARDNER graduated from the University of Michigan and served with the Signal Intelligence on Okinawa and Korea during World War II. After the war he was on the staff of the *New Yorker* for seven years. From 1955 to 1957 he was the chief comedy writer for Ernie Kovacs. (In 1955 the show won the Sylvania Award for Creative Television Technique.) His humorous streak has also revealed itself in two adult fiction books, *Out of the Bunker and Into the Trees* and *The Lardner Report.* Since 1961 the author has been a writer with *Sports Illustrated.* Mr. Lardner, his wife, and three children live in Great Neck, New York.